Northwick Park

A Few Shiny Bits of English History of Possible Interest to Magpies and Bowerbirds

Northwick Park

A Few Shiny Bits of English History of Possible Interest to
Magpies and Bowerbirds

Richard A. Bertocci

Published in the United Kingdom by
Blockley Heritage Society
Blockley Heritage Centre, Park Road, Blockley GL56 9BY

Registered office: The Old Bakery, High Street, Blockley, Gloucestershire GL5 9EU
Incorporated in England as a company limited by guarantee number 7008626 and registered as a
charity number 1133319.

First edition published 2014

ISBN 978-0-9563738-6-1
British Library Cataloguing in Publication Data:
A catalogue record of this book is available from the British Library

Printed and bound in the UK by Berforts Information Press, Stevenage.

CONTENTS

FOREWORD

Richard Bertocci is a remarkable man. As a New York lawyer specialising in real estate, commercial law and international business law, it may have been only a matter of time before business visits to the UK led him to find a home here in the Cotswolds at Northwick Park. What is more unusual is the curiosity that prompted him to research the history of the place. But perhaps that is not so surprising for a lawyer specialising in real estate. A desire to investigate must be a natural component of every lawyer's DNA.

The Blockley Heritage Society first became aware of Ric's interest in the history of Northwick Park through the friendship he formed with the late John Haggart, a valued member of the Society who was equally interested in researching the history of local people and local buildings–not least Blockley Parish Church. Later, a preliminary draft of this book was made available on the internet with an invitation to the public to comment on it. It is a mark of Ric's generosity and his respect for John Haggart that proceeds from visits to the website were donated to the Church.

With plans evolving for a permanent Heritage Centre in Blockley, the Society quickly recognised that there was likely to be a continuing demand for Ric's detailed account of the history of Northwick Park and its owners. We are therefore delighted that he has agreed to allow the Society to publish the work. We are also very appreciative of the technical contribution made by Ric's son Adam towards the production of the book.

It is a fascinating account. We hope you will enjoy it.

Robert Willott
Chairman
Summer 2014

PREFACE

Our son threatened to hang a sign on our little house at Northwick: "On this spot on January 23, 1693 nothing happened." He can't do that because he can't be sure nothing happened, and, more to the point, the Mansion is landmarked, Grade I listed, and no one can alter its appearance one iota without the approval of teams of preservationist bureaucrats. Yet, I digress. (Get used to it.)

Whether we can find out whether something notable happened in Northwick on January 23, 1693 goes to the heart of the organizational problem in this little book. The records are skimpy. When I found out that something did happen, the chances were that I had no idea what it meant so I had to look that up too. So I ended up with a pile of notes and a first draft in which the footnotes were more interesting than the text. There was no grand theme and no ending; I simply ran out of interesting bits. Realizing that the shiny bits buried in the notes were more interesting than the nest, like a bowerbird I have tried to arrange them to attract your interest.

This is a book to rummage in; if a chapter is a bore, skip it. All that hangs this book together is that it tells part of what happened in this one place sometime in the last thousand years or so and attempts to shed some light on some of the more obscure economic, social and legal developments which informed the events. My style is that of a magpie: 'Oh, I like that bit, I'll have that.' I digress, and digress again from the digression. If a part of my bower does not interest you, find one that does.

A warning: Northwick is not great architecture and its owners were not all that interesting or, on the whole, very nice. But in the right light, bits of it glitter.

And a suggestion: Critical background information was put in the appendices so as not to overwhelm a casual reader or bore those who know more than I do. Reading the first appendix on the legal context will help most readers and you won't lose your will to live before you finish it; it's only two pages and may encourage you to read later appendices when their topics arise.

A disclaimer: The Blockley Heritage Society has kindly published this edition as a service to the community, but I alone am responsible for its contents.

Finally, a note of thanks: You would not be reading this had my son Adam not imposed some structure on what had been an accumulation of notes. He was not entirely successful but given what he had to work with you too should be grateful for his efforts. Adam also did what he could with the photos and the layout in Word. My wife Danielle declines to be thanked for tolerating my spending endless hours in archives and libraries; her view is that it kept me off the streets and out of the bars and was probably for the good.

John Haggart led the way in Rushout research and generously guided me, shared his notes and thoughts, and was a friend who will be missed. He published his work to assist others and I am trying to follow his example.

Richard A. Bertocci
September 2014

NORTHWICK PARK

A Few Shiny Bits of English History of Possible Interest to Magpies and Bowerbirds

There were over 3000 wounded down there. The hospital spanned 72 acres of the Northwick estate. All forces were there, soldiers, sailors, airmen and not just the Americans. The German surgeons were operating at night and the Americans in the day.[1]

WHAT? In my back yard? Within my lifetime? What was this about?

On page 100 I'll tell you what it was about but first let me orient you: Western England. Fifty miles from southern Wales and twenty miles northwest of Oxford, a twenty-five-square-mile district of hills known as the Cotswolds. Scholars quibble about the derivation and meaning of 'Cotswolds', but I like the version "high sheep meadows", because that is what they have been and to a significant extent remain. This is picture-book England; thatched roofs and honeyed limestone.

The Northwick estate was a 2000-acre farm, which has had its own identity for a thousand years. It lies between Chipping Campden, a 16th-century town preserved as if in amber, and Blockley, a predominantly 18th-century hill town. Both villages made it into the Domesday Book, documenting an antiquity still in evidence.

Chipping Campden

---

[1] Quote from E. Hicks at http://www.cotswold.gov.uk/nqcontent.cfm?a_id=1748

Blockley

       "Northwick" meant a large farm or settlement north of somewhere and the 'somewhere' in this case was Blockley. The center of the estate, which came to be known as Northwick Park, was a predominantly 16th-century Mansion with various outbuildings, including a coach house. In the 1970s the Mansion, its outbuildings and about thirty-five acres of land were split from the rest of the estate and redeveloped as residences. My wife and I bought a little piece of the coach house, a short walk from where we later learned there had been a huge army field hospital during World War II, which also serviced one of the largest POW camps in England a couple of miles away. But I get ahead of myself.

The Mansion and outbuildings

TALES OF TWO AUCTIONS

If Northwick is not an architectural masterpiece, if most of its buildings are not very old and if no one important ever lived there, then why has anyone even heard of it? Because Northwick is famous for what is no longer there: two of the world's great private art collections, which were auctioned off about a hundred years apart. The men who assembled these collections, a pompous peer in the 19th century and a soldier, the grandson of a Duke, in the 20th century, are worth study as extinct species whose lives and times glitter a bit.

Wander through some of the world's leading museums and in the provenance of some of the gems you will see "Northwick sale, 1859". That auction attracted huge attention, as it was the largest dispersal of great works of art since the collection of Charles I was liquidated by the Puritans. About twelve hundred paintings went on the block over twenty-two days. The paintings were attributed to the very top rank of European artists: Rembrandt, da Vinci, Rubens, Rafael, Holbein, Reynolds, Gainsborough, Titian, Van Dyke, Giotto, and dozens of others.

Before the date of the sale in 1859, art history was unscientific and largely the province of amateur connoisseurs who made outlandish guesses. We could surmise that half the attributions of works in the collection were flat-out wrong or at least merited demotion to "circle of". We should further accept that standards of conservation and restoration were dismal. Many of the paintings were very old, on panels or deteriorating canvas, and had been transported by sailing ship and oxcart from temperate central Italy to damp England. So we can guess that a third of them, even if correctly attributed, were in a condition no better than pub signs. Yet that still leaves hundreds of paintings of the very first rank. It is difficult to identify many of the paintings now because the 1859 sale catalog was terse, did not give dimensions or specify the medium or surface, used titles which may not still be in use, and of course there is the misattribution problem. But still, the quality is amazing. This portrait was catalogued as by Massacio:

It now hangs in the National Gallery in London as the work of Sandro Botticelli.

This Botticelli was correctly catalogued.

It is now in the National Galleries of Scotland having been "given" by the heirs of the buyer for the remission of £10,250,000 in death duties.

This painting was auctioned as Giorgione. The Wallace Collection has it ascribed to Titian. It's one of many paintings that Lord Hertford, the founder of the Collection, purchased at the Northwick sale, ten of which still hang in the museum today.

This painting is now in the Detroit Institute of the Arts as a Sassetta—

—but it was sold in 1959 as a Giotto. There were ten Giotto attributions in the 1859 sale; that seems to have been the default attribution for anything with statue-like figures.

So identifying the art can be difficult. For example, I was personally interested in tracking down the three Hogarths. One, *Portrait of Dr. Locke*, is in the Johnson Museum at Cornell. A second, *Midnight Modern Conversation*, is not the one in the Mellon collection at Yale; Yale knows the Northwick version exists but does not know where it is. Yet a third, auctioned in 1859 as *The Hazard Table*, is… who knows where? A very boring engraving by that name exists, attributed (wrongly) to Hogarth, but I have no idea what it was copied from.

You may need to poke around to find the provenances but the dispersed Northwick collection is everywhere. The Met in New York has ten. The National Gallery of Art in Washington has five. And that's just paintings. A huge number of coins, medallions, sculptures, and antiquities were sold as well and they are in collections all over the world.

That was the first Northwick sale. The second occurred one hundred and six years later.

Again, as you wander in great museums, spot the legend "Spencer-Churchill Collection" or "Northwick sale, 1965". The last heir to Northwick was Captain Edward George Spencer-Churchill who inherited Northwick and most of its contents including the four hundred or so paintings that Lord George Rushout, heir to the deceased collector, Lord John Rushout, bought in 1859. Captain Churchill (he never used the 'Spencer') collected another two hundred or so paintings. He specialized in highly speculative purchases of paintings so encrusted with dirt and varnish that their merit and condition could not be determined. He would have them cleaned and restored, and took great pride in his successes—so much so that he entitled the catalogue of these relics *The Northwick Rescues, 1912-1961*. On the Captain's death, his painting collection was brought down to Christie's King Street for sales in May, June and October 1965 and February 1966. Again it is difficult to identify and trace most of the pictures. Some may still be in private hands and unpublished; certainly some were misattributed. For instance, a picture called *Peasant*

Wedding, said to be by Pieter Breugel the Elder, which had been bought-in for either 21 or 40 guineas in 1859 (depending on which alleged Breugel in the 1859 catalogue it was) brought the highest price in the 1965 sale: 78,000 guineas (multiply by 12.86 to get that in 2005 pounds) even though the catalogue was frank to acknowledge scholarly doubts about its attribution. There are several Breugel *Peasant Weddings* and this was not the most famous of them, which features two men carrying a pallet of pies in the lower right–I still cannot find the Northwick version. This painting illustrates the problem of tracing the works. Even in the 1965 sale catalogue it was called *A Peasant Wedding* by Pieter Brueghel the Elder. Now it is called *Peasant Wedding Procession* by Pieter Brueghel the Younger. There are quite a number of versions around, including in museums in Worcester, Massachusetts and Brussels. What strikes me as a quite inferior copy sold at Sotheby's London in 2007 for about $2.7 million and the buyer, a London dealer, reportedly re-sold it to an American collector in 2010 for $4.5 million. There is a fairly decent color illustration of Churchill's copy in the 1965 catalogue, and it looks to be vastly better than the others, which tend to have a Disney look to them. Though it's a minor complication in the search, the Elder dropped the 'h' from his name in 1559 ten years before his death; the Younger kept it. The Younger was a much less talented painter and I've wondered whether he is indeed the painter of the inferior copies of the *Wedding Procession,* copied from his father.

Another Breugel, *Rest on the Flight into Egypt*, brought 12,000 guineas in 1965 and is now in the Kunsthistorisches Museum in Vienna.

It is fascinating to line up the prices at which Lord George Rushout bought-in paintings in 1859 with the sale prices they achieved in 1965, but the bottom line is that you buy contemporary art at your peril, at least if you are a Victorian. Among the paintings sold in the Churchill sale was *Lot and His Daughter,* which had been bought as a Velasquez in 1859 for 140 guineas but sold in 1965 for 38,000 guineas. It is now in the Getty as a Gentileschi. Guido Reni's *Angel Appearing to St. Jerome* (350 guineas in 1859 and 22,000 guineas in 1965) is now in the Detroit Institute of Art and *Adoration of the Magi* sold as a Van Eyck in 1859 for 172 guineas but is now at the Met in New York as by Gerard David having been sold for 26,000 guineas in 1965. An alleged Fra Angelico of Saints Cosmas and Damian which Lord John Rushout bought for £21.12s.6d and Lord George Rushout bought in for 74

guineas was sold in 1965 for 13,500 guineas but I cannot trace it. It was alleged to be the only Fra Angelico in private hands. I wonder if it too has been re-attributed. Rather than continue to track the re-sales from 1859, let me give two examples of things the Captain himself acquired.

He bought this *Madonna and Child* by Dirk Bouts from Sotheby's in 1935. I do not know where it is now. Conversely, I do not know where or when Captain Churchill bought this little bronze, but I know where it is: on its own pedestal in the middle of a principal ground floor corridor of the British Museum.

This bronze is one of about 425 items that the British Museum has with the Captain's provenance. Many are prints, but there are a vast number of curious smalls, little bronzes, scarabs, and coins all of great antiquity–all collected by the Captain himself. In addition to the paintings, in 1965 and 1966 there were four separate auctions of Indian miniatures and books and one of silver.

I will come back to the subject of the auctions later and provide some local color, gossip and scandal, but first let's consider the question of how it could happen that two great collections were suddenly dispersed.

Collectors are to a greater or lesser degree fanatics. Some are assemblers who simply want to obtain a good example of every one in a series of stamps, comic books or whatever, and when the chase is over, they are quite happy to sell off the collection because the passion was in the chase. Art and antique collectors tend to be different; they have to have a particular object and having obtained it, they care about what happens to it and view it as part of their personal legacy. Some are jealous and cannot bear to think of someone else possessing the cherished object. Others think of themselves as temporary custodians and agonize about how to pass an object on in case God does not let them take it with them. Either way, eventual disposition of the objects is a serious concern for them. So it is remarkable that the two great Northwick collections were simply disposed of at public auctions. To try to see why this happened without a bankruptcy or untimely death, we should consider the personalities of the two great collectors.

JOHN RUSHOUT V,
2nd Baron Northwick, The First Collector

We start with John Rushout who assembled the first collection. I will occasionally refer to him as Lord John (though that is technically an improper form of address) or John V, because a long but non-consecutive line of Johns and a couple of James feature in this story. (There's a table at the end of this book that may help you keep things straight.) He was the fifth generation in a family that had owned Northwick since 1683, of whom you will hear more anon. At this point all you need to know is that they were rich and that through much of the 17th and 18th centuries they were minor members of Parliament.

At the age of twenty-three in 1792, John V left for Spain; he was in Italy by September 1793. Except for six months spent in Germany, Switzerland and Austria, he seems to have been in Italy until 1800, obsessively collecting Renaissance medallions and ancient coins. Another English traveler met up with him in Naples in 1795 and found him with a collection "upwards of twelve thousand, and he gives up his whole time to it from morning to night".

John Rushout by Angelica Kauffman, Rome, 1794.

Along the way, John picked up a valet-factotum, Louis Mayland, who stayed with him all his life arranging his travels and shipping things, but apparently at some level also being a friend and companion–a sort of Jeeves and Wooster team, perhaps. Accommodation in Italian hostelries at that time was limited so occasionally they had to sleep two to a bed. John was a bachelor, passionate about art, with a lifelong male companion. There is no evidence of women in his life. But don't jump to conclusions just yet. During this period for a man of means this was not unusual–traveling, managing multiple houses, *etc.*, was not easy and having someone who could be trusted to handle all the dreary details of life and whose company was bearable was a nice benefit of being wealthy. More on this later.

It is probably coincidence that John returned to England in September 1800, about six weeks before his father's death and his succession to the titles. John became a governor of the Harrow School in 1801, an almost hereditary post since his great-great grandfather married Alice Pitt, the heiress to the Manor of Harrow-on-the-Hill (much more on that later). It is because of this lord-of-the-manor connection that we have a Northwick Park Hospital at Harrow-on-the-Hill and a Northwick Park station nearby on the London Underground.

But John did not directly succeed to Northwick. His mother Rebecca received Northwick directly from John's father, John IV, even though it was "entailed"–restricted to be inherited by the oldest living son of the then-current owner.[2] John's father gave Northwick to his wife, Rebecca, by a lifetime gift and gave her another large property by will so clearly these "first son to first son" restrictions were not bulletproof.

Here is how John's mother, Rebecca, got Northwick. Bear with me because it's complicated but becomes interesting. John's father's father's (John III) will, dated March 29, 1771, gave John's father the ability to carve out a twenty-year grant of Northwick plus a right to mortgage property for up to £10,000 to protect John IV's wife and children other than his eldest son. John III died in March 1775; his son, John V's father, had married Rebecca in June 1766 and John V was born on February 16, 1769.

Now the timing becomes interesting. John IV could have protected his wife Rebecca and younger children on the death of his father in 1775, but he did not. It was not until November 26, 1785, when John V was 16 years old, that his father chose to settle "the Manor of Northwick" and the "capital Mansion house or manor house at Northwick" and all of his property in the Parish of Blockley on Rebecca for life.[3] He gave other estates to trustees for the younger children. Then in his will dated February 15, 1786 (less than three months after making the settlement on Rebecca) John V's father gave Rebecca everything else within his powers of disposition with the right to give it to any of her children other than any eldest son.[4] Now it may be that because so much property was entailed to his son that John IV was just trying to do well by the wife and younger children but I doubt it. At around the time John IV made this will, he shipped John V off to the Continent for reasons that are not clear and John stayed there until June 1789, when he went back to England for about a year, perhaps driven home by the reactions in revolutionary France. By August 1790, John V was headed back to Europe, where he remained for the next nine years.

John V made handwritten notes in the margins of a copy of the January 11, 1793 codicil to his father's will noting that the original 1786 will was executed "When I was in Switzerland". Since the purpose of the codicil was to state that property acquired by the testator after the date of the original will was to follow the scheme of the original will as at that time it was not clear that a will devised after-acquired property, John V noted "estates purchased since 11th January 1793 not devised" and he noted that "I was 24 yrs [illegible]". I read that as 'The old bastard cut me out and kept cutting me out but there may be some leavings if he acquired property after 11 January 1793.'

---

[2] Primogeniture as practiced in England simply passed the property to the oldest son by operation of law and, before 1540, you could not do otherwise. However, with the passage of the Statute of Wills in 1540, it was possible to make something called a "testament" which could cut out the oldest son entirely. Entailment is another way in which the succession to property was controlled and it occurs when the grantor of real estate provides that the real estate being transferred goes to the grantee and "the heirs of his body", meaning his lawful progeny in successive generations. Entailment was harder to break using a fictitious lawsuit called a "recovery" but it could be done. If you did not break the entail, you could also grant the entailed property to someone else but on your death, the property would revert to your successor who could kick out your grantee.

[3] John II's will authorized a grant for twenty years, but John III granted it for Rebecca's life.

[4] I have no confidence that I have fully understood the details of the various wills, leases, settlements and other legal documents I describe in this tome, but I do think I come close enough for these purposes.

At any rate, John V succeeded to the title but mommy copped the lot[5] and kept it until she died in 1818.

There is a stunning aspect of Rebecca's will; she never mentions her eldest son affectionately. She refers repeatedly to her "dear daughter Anne Rushout", her "dear little granddaughter Georgina Rushout", "my dear brother George Bowles", "my dear daughter Harriet", "my dear daughter Elizabeth", *etc*. She constantly calls her late husband "my dear Lord". John is identified as "my son John Lord Northwick" or "the person or persons who for the time being is in possession" of Northwick. The reason for this latter impersonality may be a recognition that the estate was entailed and that she wanted the property in question to go to follow the entailment of Northwick. The mother and son may not have been on the best terms (she lived at Northwick, the son was either in London or Harrow) but there is evidence of a thaw. In Rebecca's June 19, 1809 will she first let John buy the contents of Northwick and "Pair of Earings, Two large Stars for the Hair and Necklace consisting of 36 Brilliants" for £6,000, but if he declined that offer, the property was to be auctioned with the proceeds to go into trust for the younger children. She revoked the provision by second codicil to her will years later and the jewelry was given outright to John V.

The critical aspect of Rebecca's will, however, is that she did not exercise the power which her husband granted to her to leave Northwick to her other children–so when she died, it passed to her son John V under the entailment. This must have been no surprise as John was getting involved in estate matters before Rebecca's death. In 1803 he commented on the proposed text of his mother's renewals of the leases of large parts of the estate of which the Rushouts were tenants (accusing the landlord of slipping in some unprecedented conditions) and on February 17, 1815, John wrote to the landlord offering to buy the land subject to the leases.

Upon Rebecca's death in 1818, Lord John had title to and possession of his seat. He continued to travel and collect assiduously. Some of his diaries from the 1850s are at the University of London Library (mis-catalogued as being those of his sister Anne); they are brief notes of where he had been and what he had seen without editorializing or revealing much.

I am not clear as to when Lord John began to collect paintings seriously. He was collecting coins and medallions during the years he spent in Europe before his father's death but while he must have had a generous allowance from his father (possibly having the status of a remittance man–paid to stay away) he would not have had a large disposable income at least until his father died and probably not until his mother died. He did buy paintings in Italy, including a Titian which he picked up cheap from an impoverished Italian nobleman in 1795, and in 1799 he acquired Schidone's *Children with the Hornbook* and an Etruscan vase which he recognized as having been stolen from the Royal Palace in Naples. He bought the two items for a "trifle" from a "mean looking dwelling" of the likely thief but somehow did not see fit to return them to his hosts, the King and Queen of Naples.

---

[5] The historian of Rebecca's family, the Bowles, says estrangement ensued with John living mainly on the continent collecting pictures until his mother died in 1818–but that is not true. Indeed, family legend has it that John never saw his mother again after his father died, which is also not true. It also says Northwick was given to Rebecca as part of her marriage settlement. That is clearly not true. See *Records of the Bowles Family* by William Henry Bowles, Derby, London, 1918.

As a consequence of the French revolution and the Napoleonic wars, London was flooded with art from the Continent around the time that Lord John was collecting. And collect he did. He filled his house in Connaught Place in London with pictures by 1830, and in 1832 put a wing on Northwick to house more pictures. That was not enough, so by 1839 he acquired a large Greek-revival house in Cheltenham, a fashionable Georgian spa about twenty miles west of Northwick, which he enlarged adding successive wings of galleries to house his collection. This house was called Thirlestane and, extraordinarily, it was open to the public for three hours most afternoons. It became an important local institution and it was believed (or at least hoped) that Lord John would leave Thirlestane and its contents to the town as a museum.[6]

The 1859 auction was conducted at Thirlestane and the art at Northwick was shipped there to be part of the sale, presumably because a large part of the collection was already in Cheltenham but probably more importantly, the bidders needed somewhere to stay for a month or so and Cheltenham as a spa had suitable accommodation.

Like many who acquire art on a massive scale, Lord John tried a few times to thin out his collection and on May 12, 1838 he sold works of "modern artists" at Christie's (but failed to sell Hogarth's *Midnight Modern Conversation* and *The Hazard Table,* which were both re-offered in the 1859 sale). Then over three days starting on May 24, 1838 he auctioned Old Masters from his house in Connaught Place, also without great success as most of the paintings were still on offer in 1859.

His sales attracted the ire of London dealers who were threatened by the competition and did what dealers have always done: they micturated on his goods. A weekly paper, the *Athanaeum*, hissed:

> The sale of Lord Northwick's collection, which took place last week at Christie & Manson's, has been an affair much more curious than comprehensible. Many works advertised in the Catalogue were not to be seen in the auction-room; and of those sent, many were either not allowed to be sold at all, or sold back to the seller himself. But farther: an opulent nobleman purchases at several times and places so many paintings, within so short a period, to sell them again forthwith, that picture-dealers begin to doubt whether a right honourable rival have got among them; and by drawing up his own catalogue in the most fulsome and florid style of panegyric, auctioneers likewise begin to tremble for their supremacy in puffing. We do believe his lordship "much too wise to walk into a well," but this attempt on the

---

[6] In what could be viewed as a grand act of toadying, a group of seven hundred noblemen and gentlemen of Cheltenham and the surrounding neighborhood presented Lord John with a bound citation thanking him for permitting Thirlestane House to be open to the public. It was a massive volume with covers of carved ebony on a deep crimson velvet ground carrying busts of Cimabue, Michelangelo, Raphael and Cellini in silver gilt with decorative cartouches and interlacing strapwork surrounding in the center the arms of Cheltenham above the presentation inscription to Lord Northwick. At the opening of the 1859 sale, the auctioneer, Mr. Phillips, announced that because Lord George as administrator of the estate had a duty to liquidate everything, this volume would be auctioned, but that Lord George would be making a preemptive bid on the item. In other words, he asked the bidders to sit on their hands as a courtesy to the family. In the event, there was a bid of 1 guinea, then 5 guineas, and then Lord George bid 100 guineas. In 1965, this homage to John V went off the block for 7 guineas.

bombastic Muse is certainly not the most sagacious part of his conduct: it exposes to the severest animadversion either his connoisseurship or his candour. Is the noble proprietor, indeed, a dilettante so simple as to mistake that piece of fuddled grotesque, the *Diana and Acteon*, for a Cranach, or the *Magdalen* for a Leonardo, the *Danaë* for a Titian, &c. &c.? Even a blind amateur could almost tell by the feel, that a coarse thing called *Mademoiselle Lundens*, veritable pitch-painting, was no Rubens–the *Two Lovers* no Raffael–the *Children*, so bethumped with compliments by the Catalogue, no Schedone. In short, there were few–very few pictures of much account in the collection; and we apprehend the shallowest busybody that flits round objects of virtù, must have discovered the fact, though, perhaps, not to its full extent.

But having said that in four column inches, the writer went on for fourteen column inches to debate the attributions of a large number of admittedly wonderful paintings. From this distance all we can conclude is that Lord John probably believed his own nonsense and made more than his share of errors, but had a really good eye for a fine painting.

Lord John had a distinctly nasty, self-righteous and litigious side. There is one reported court case of interest. In *Lord Northwick v. Stanway* 3 Bos. & Pul. 346, 127 ER 189, John V tried to injure a tenant by fixing an above-market rent for the record but agreeing to take less. The court directed that the lower amount be recorded as the amount due as "mischief might arise" if landlords could get away with recording higher rent levels than were in fact justified and then informally taking less.

John V even got into a long-running squabble with the Blockley vicar over the appointment of a master for the church school, which created a situation in which the vicar's nominee held forth on the ground floor while John's man reigned on the first floor.[7]

In the 1830s, Lord John was much criticized for sitting as a magistrate in the trial of the criminal case brought against his own farm manager and workers whom he had sent to dismantle a threshing machine used by one of his tenants. John V had feared that the machine would attract the attention of marauding bands of farm workers who were resisting the industrial revolution in an energetic fashion by destroying farm machinery, burning barns, *etc.* The scathing press attention he received because he sat as a magistrate in the trial of his own staff who acted at his direction caused John to publish a pamphlet in his own defense, which shows how self-righteous and obtuse he was. The pamphlet consists largely of an exchange of correspondence between John and William Boughton, vicar of Blockley who was also a magistrate on the panel. Lord Northwick argues that there was no crime because he ordered his men to remove the thresher

---

[7] There is another recorded case involving John. He acquired the extensive family estates at Harrow on his mother's death and there appears to have been some sort of enclosure which resulted in several people, including Rushout, purchasing the enclosed land from three commissioners. Rushout purchased 9 acres, 3 rods, 37 perch of "land in front of the Mansion house and land" for £750 (a very large amount of money). Another of the purchasers brought suit in the equity courts against the commissioners, who officiated on the enclosure, complaining of how they executed their duties, which, if true, would mean that that Rushout got something he shouldn't have gotten. Three iterations of the complaint and two answers are in the National Archive as document C 13/106/25. I don't know what the outcome was.

from his tenant's barn and while in law he was responsible for their acts, he was telling his own people what to do on his own property so of course he could not be guilty of a crime and therefore they could not be guilty of a crime. The language John uses to the vicar is abusive: "What, Sir is there no character at stake, no Honour to be upheld but your own? Is it immaterial that I be held up to public execration, be dragged from my hereditary seat on the Magisterial Bench to be plunged into the Felons dock, and threatened many similar outrages, all calculated to excite a deluded and infuriated populace to acts of spoliation and murder?" The magistrates decided to refer the matter to Lord Melbourne, the Home Secretary, for a ruling on whether they were right to hear the case. Melbourne, who had earlier sent out a directive telling magistrates to come down hard both on people who were destroying machinery and those who were removing it to avoid the wrath of the laborers (*e.g.* Lord Northwick) declined jurisdiction by writing on the back of the envelope containing the inquiry from the magistrates "there appears to me to be no doubt that the Magistrates have acted right in this case and Lord Northwick was wrong–but it does not appear to me to be part of my duty to pronounce any decision as between them, particularly upon the absurd altercation which took place." Anyway, John's men were convicted, heavily fined and Northwick paid the fines plus costs. It could have been worse–the offences with which they were charged, riotous assembly, were capital offences.

John succeeded to the Lordship of the Manor of Harrow and, as his rights and duties in that capacity were less than clear-cut, he spent a lot of time and money fighting his corner. John chose to fight over the issue of whether his rights of his "Small Tithes" of "pulse and herbage" (beans, tares and vetches–clover and fodder) were cut off when the burdened land was distributed under the Harrow Enclosure Act. The sums involved could not have been significant but John wanted to make his case until counsel advised him it was a loser.

More interesting, however, was John's litigation to protect his claim as lord of the manor to the property of an executed murderer. In 1813, one Thomas Bowler shot and killed a man. Bowler's property as a matter of law became the property of his overlord but the question was: Which lord? The Lord of the Manor or the King? The incidents of the Lordship of Manor were less than crystal clear. A massive inventory of Bowler's property was made–eighteen pages of detail running from large amounts of land to £1159 and 18 pence of goods and chattels counting everything down to pots and pans. John's claim was that by virtue of a grant made by King Edward IV dated 15th of April in the second year of his reign (1463) and several prior grants therein mentioned and also by virtue of a grant made by Henry VIII bearing the date of the 5th of January in the thirty-seventh year of his reign (1546), the Lord of the Manor of Harrow was entitled to Bowler's property as Bowler was a tenant "within the manor who may be convicted of felony, attainted, outlawed or adjuged to die at the suit of the King or of the King and others." John wrote to the Lords Commissioners of His Majesty's Treasury asking for their help in securing his rights. As late as 1817 Rushout was still squabbling in a long legal letter soliciting the help of Lord Redesdale to get a hearing in the Court of Exchequer. The Exchequer eventually ruled that John as the lord of the manor could only claim Bowler's goods and chattels within the manor; Bowler seems to have had property outside the manor.

In fairness it seems that John was simply trying to vindicate a principle and he turned over his recovery, net of his expenses (which must have been massive) to Bowler's family. But it is clear, especially in his letter to Redesdale, that John was acutely aware of the value of his feudal rights and was not going to give an inch.

Another unpleasant image of John V emerges from the memoirs of a Victorian artist by the name of W.P. Frith who at the age of 25, having been an associate of the Royal Academy for two years, visited Northwick in 1846 when John was 77. Frith was clearly an arrogant young twerp and admits that he behaved badly on the visit mocking his host but he clearly thought that his contempt for the elderly Baron was well deserved.

After commenting that Northwick's collection "was filled with very questionable old masters", Frith launches into a portrait of the old man as a posturer:

> At the time of our visit to Cheltenham, the corn-law question was raging with great fury, and Lord Northwick made such long and tiresome speeches to us on the subject that we often wished him in the House of Lords, where his eloquence, strange to say, was never heard. He almost wept over the imminent ruin of the farmers, and the possible reduction of all rents; and his words, 'Protection to native industry,' repeated again and again in a singing tone [were repeated over the years by a mimic who was one of Frith's party].[8]

One more glimpse of Lord John: He apparently wrote rudely to his landlord, the Bishop of Worcester, on the subject of renewing the leases. A response dated March 14, 1837 from Hartlebury Castle addressed to Lord Northwick reads:

> As your Lordship is pleased to address me in a language to which as a Gentleman, I am not accustomed, I must beg leave to decline all further correspondence with you. If your Lordship should be desirous to renew your Leases, I must request you will make your intentions known through your Agent to Mr. S. Clifton of Worcester. I have the Honor to be, My Lord, Your Lordship's very humble servant RJ Worcester.

By November 1839, John and the Bishop seem to have come to terms but the Vicar of Blockley became the obstacle as he was holding out for an advance of 10% of the rectorial tithes (tithes were separate from, but measured by, rent and, like rents, and could be discounted) and the deal got in trouble because, as John's agent said, "This might have been arranged but Lord Northwick and the Vicar are not friends and neither are inclined to give way."

Extraordinarily, John V died without a will in 1859. This is utterly bizarre. It is not that John was not worldly. This was a period in which people of this class devoted scrupulous care and energy to estate planning. Their wills are incredibly complicated with trusts, life estates, conditional bequests, and finely measured expressions of affection and gratitude. There was a tremendous sense of the importance of maintaining the family name and position.

How could a man such as Rushout who was so obsessive, whose pride and joy was a great art collection the disposition of which he cared about passionately (to the point of

---

[8] *My Autobiography and Reminiscences*, W.P. Frith, Harper, New York, 1888. p. 106.

considering leaving his huge house in Cheltenham as a museum to house his collection), and who had been so injured by his father's will, die intestate? It's not as if death snuck up on him–he was eighty-nine. True, he suffered a paralytic stroke two years before his death but if anything, that should have been fair warning to make a will.

I choose to see it as the ultimate expression of alienation–'To hell with all of you!'

Now we have a few more facts; maybe we are entitled to do a little bargain-basement psychiatry. The Rushouts had been rising socially for over a hundred years when John Rushout IV made a will excluding his eighteen-year-old son and heir and giving his wife the power to dole out the goodies among their other children in her will. John IV may not have been confident of the peerage that came his way in the end, but it could not have been a big surprise as he and his father, John III, had sought elevation so assiduously. Yet he cut out the heir to the cherished title. Did he have grave misgivings about his son's character? Within five years of the making of the will, the son was off to the Continent for virtually the rest of his father's life. This is not a problem with the parents–the father seems to have been a successful politician, which suggests he could handle people, and Rebecca was universally admired. John's sisters were capable of love and affection and John's brother George was a much-loved minister at Burford. No, there was something in John which heavily influenced his life and the way he left life. Why rule out the obvious? Could he have come out as gay as a teenager, been rejected by his parents and battled his way through life under a cloud? This was not a time when being homosexual was remotely acceptable; it was a felony. You could be hanged. The pieces fit, albeit inconclusively.

John V's failure to produce an heir also supports this sheer speculation. John and his forebears were obsessed with their ancient lineage and had finally attained a peerage. His sister, Anne, paid a nephew £10,000 to change his surname to Rushout so that the name would continue. Surely a marriage, if only for convenience, could have been arranged. Lord John was handsome, rich and well-connected. There was an over-supply of suitable aristocratic breeding stock around; he could have followed his grandfather and married the daughter of at least an earl if not of a marquis or a duke. He had substantial homes in London, at Harrow, Northwick and in Cheltenham so he needn't have even seen her much once her job was done. Something kept John from tending to business. It could be that his relationship with his own father was so fraught that undertaking any sort of parenting was too threatening. Or, if he was gay, he simply could not tolerate the thought of even the most minimal service in the breeding shed. I have no basis for saying this but for a man as proud as Lord John, maybe a companionate marriage, if that was all that was on offer, was too shaming and placed him too much at risk of disclosure. It was not that homosexuality was unknown in England (King James I and William III enjoyed the companionship of attractive young men) but even in the aristocracy where criminal prosecution of a reasonably discreet gay man was unlikely, it was not something you wanted to have known.

Rather than close this section on a sad note, let me tell a possibly more appealing story. There is a suggestive story in Frith's book of a very old butler at Northwick who insisted on placing the dishes on the table at dinner. "All went well so long as the burden was light, but a haunch of venison proved beyond the old man's strength; the dish–a heavy silver one–slipped from his fingers, and the venison fell upon the floor. 'He is too old,' Lord Northwick whispered to me. 'I can't bear to tell him so, dear old man. He is forever dropping something or other.'"[9] I am sure the old butler was Northwick's life-long companion, Louis Mayland. Louis died in 1853 at the age of 87 and is buried in the Blockley churchyard. His meticulous household inventories in an increasingly shaky hand show him at work faithfully for Lord John up to his death. John V was an unpleasant piece of work but he had a decent side.

[9] Frith p. 108.

THE FIRST SALE

John V was childless and his brother George, the minister at Burford, pre-deceased him in 1842, so the title passed to George's son, also named George, who had chosen to take the name Rushout-Bowles by royal license in 1817 and would become George I. John V's heirs at law were a surviving sister, Elizabeth, a niece, Georgina, and a nephew, George, who would succeed to Northwick under the entailment unless Lord John had made a will to the contrary. But clearly Lord John intended that his nephew George would inherit Northwick, as he consulted with George in the 1830s and 1840s in all matters relating to the renewal of the Bishop's leases.

Lord George, the 3rd Baron, confronted with John V's intestacy, tried to buy out his relatives' interests in the art collection to avoid liquidation. The niece made no claim but the other two haggled. Finally, about two months before the sale, they struck a deal in which Lord George guaranteed the other two £38,500 each from the sale of the art net of legacy tax and expenses. Since George I merely guaranteed minimum proceeds, the sale had to go ahead anyway.

The sale grossed £91,072 so the other heirs made a very good deal. It is not clear to me why Lord George so agreed though it seems he got some items such as books and prints in the bargain free of their claims. The prints and books were sold in 628 lots at Sotheby's in 1860 and a further 1,625 coins and medals were sold at Sotheby's in 1859. In the main sale Lord George brought in about four hundred of the fifteen hundred paintings on the block in Cheltenham, but unfortunately his taste was typical of gentlemen of the period, so he got more than his share of duds. Here is part of his shopping list:

Maclise's large painting of *Robin Hood and his Foresters*, for 1305 guineas;
The Stoning of St. Stephen, by Garofalo, 1530 guineas;
Frost's *Diana and her Nymphs Surprised by Actaeon*, 675 guineas;
Cuyp's full-length portrait of *Count Egmont*, 300 guineas;
Danby's *Wood Nymph Chanting her Hymn to the Rising Sun*, 360 guineas;
Redgrave's *Flight into Egypt*, 350 guineas;
Van Schendel's admired *Market Scene—Selling Poultry by Candle-light*, 255 guineas;
De Loutherbourg's *Avalanche*, 231 guineas;
Guercino's *Sampson and the Honeycomb*, 390 guineas;
Bellini's likeness of *Mahomet the Second*, 175 guineas;
Ruben's Gallery *The Lion Hunt*, 300 guineas;
Van der Capella's *Marine View—a Calm*, 186 guineas;
Landscape with Three Horses, by A. Cuyp, 145 guineas;
A Scene in Canterbury Meadows, by T.S. Cooper, 125 guineas;
G. Dow's *Portrait of Dr. Harvey*, 120 guineas;
Velasquez' *Lot and his Daughters*, 140 guineas.

The hammer prices in the auction were all in guineas, which was an English gold coin that was supposed to be the equivalent of one pound sterling, but as the value of gold changed, it became worth more than one pound and its purchasing power varied accordingly. In 1717 its price was set to be 1 pound and 1 shilling (there being 20 shillings in a pound). The guinea disappeared from circulation after 1816, but transactions having an upper-class association such as custom tailoring, land prices, professional fees and art auction prices were all traditionally stated in guineas. Even today, after the English currency was decimalized in 1971, horse-racing prizes are still stated in guineas and now a guinea is 1 pound and 5 pence. So what did a guinea buy in 1859?

Converting historic currency to modern values is fraught; the method I prefer is purchasing power and the source I prefer is www.nationalarchives.gov.uk/currency. Though on a straight conversion, a pound in 1859 would cost about £43 in 2005, more interesting is that in 1859 a skilled craftsman in the building trades would work for less than half a pound a day or about £125 a year so that if a picture sold for £125 at the auction in 1859, you could say that a skilled craftsman would have to work six days a week for a year to earn that amount.

I refer to the auction prices in guineas so that as exchange values change after this text is published, you can re-adjust the prices to your satisfaction. In early 2014, a pound was worth about $1.60, so an American reader could read the prices as 100 guineas equals £4,400 or about $7,000 which might equate to, say, a wage of about $100,000 in late 2010. Brits can use a rule of thumb that 100 guineas at this 1859 auction would be about £4,400 or a wage of about £65,000 today. Regard both calculations as merely indicative, because while I appreciate that historic comparative purchasing power has to be based on commodity prices, including commodity labor for which prices can be found in both periods, I have a feeling that items such as art or land, which have a scarcity value, may not move in parallel with, say, the price of fleeces, wheat or the wages of farmhands. Indeed, the National Archives cautions that its calculations are merely a "general guide to historic values."

The Maclise sold for 650 guineas in the 1965 sale and reappeared at Sotheby's in 2002 with an estimate of £300,000-£400,000 and, I think, ended up in a Robin Hood Museum in Nottingham.

I have not been able to trace the Garofalo and wonder if it has been re-attributed.

The *Diana* was by William Edward Frost, a Royal Academician and the quintessential Victorian tit painter. The Victorians got their jollies from these classically themed scenes of lovely nudes or views of the harem and similar cultural studies. I have been unable to trace the picture.

The Bellini is in the National Gallery but reduced to "attributed to."

I cannot locate the Velazquez but the Guercino of *Samson and the Honeycomb* is in the de Yong Memorial Museum in San Francisco.

I have not been able to trace the Richard Redgrave but he was a typical romantic, a forgettable and forgotten Royal Academician.

The Ruben's *Lion Hunt* is in The National Gallery in London.

The Cuyp *Landscape* sold for £18,125 at Christie's in 2009 having been sold at Captain Churchill's Sale in 1966 for 1,800 guineas.

Francis Danby's *Wood Nymph* is now in the Tate as is DeLoutherbourg's *Avalanche.*

Van Schendel's *Market Scene* was for sale in a London gallery in November 2010.

The T.S. Cooper was sold for £12,900 in 2009.

The G. Dow *Portrait of Dr. Harvey* eludes me, but it may be yet another copy (at least six exist) of a lost Lely of Dr. William Harvey. (The artist's name may be Gerrit or Gerard Dou or Douw, thus illustrating the obstacles to tracing his work.)

Other than the general marked depreciation of the Victorian works, there is no pattern in what gained or lost value. The most expensive painting in the 1859 sale, Lot 1695 at 2010 guineas, was a picture of St. John by Carlo Dolci which sold at Christies in 1995 for $398,500, a modest appreciation but actually negative if you count the time value of money over a hundred years. By contrast, this Piero di Cosimo seems to have sold for less than 20 guineas in 1859 but today it is in the St. Louis Art Museum.

These paintings and hundreds of others formed the core of the collection of the next great Northwick collector, Captain Churchill, and stayed "in the family" for another hundred years or so.

CAPTAIN EDWARD GEORGE SPENCER-CHURCHILL[10]
The Second Collector

The last heir to the Northwick fortune and properties, Captain Churchill, went to Eton and Magdalene and was in the Grenadier Guards as a second lieutenant and then a lieutenant in the Boer War, winning two medals and seven "clasps"–bars recognizing service in particular battles. The Boers were the descendants of Dutch settlers in what we now call South Africa, which was annexed as a British colony in 1806. There was always tension between the Boers and the British and after the Boers declared themselves independent in 1880, relations deteriorated. In the spring of 1899 the British sent troops to protect British subjects and war was declared on October 11, 1899. Mafeking (under the command of Colonel Baden-Powell, who later founded the Boy Scouts) was besieged on October 15, starting the first great crisis.

Churchill had enlisted in April 1899 and wrote a detailed diary of his experiences in the Boer War. The diary consists of three little books, each about 3" x 5" x ¾". He thought enough of them that when he got home, he had a typescript made of them (thank goodness–his handwriting was awful) and on his death, he left the diary and copies of the typescripts to his regiment where they can be found in the regimental headquarters of the Grenadier Guards in London. The diaries are not, perhaps, of tremendous historical importance but they are very interesting as a snapshot of an experience, a time and a place.

The diary starts on January 2, 1890 and the entry for January 3 is "At Southampton. Father, Mother Ruby, Baby, Algy Rushout and Mrs. Quirk came to lunch. We sailed about 5." It is a marvelous image of the scion of an aristocratic English family lunching in uniform with his family before boarding a troop ship for a war.

The Captain did not see much action. The only three interesting bits are:

> June 12, 1900: "Marched off 8.45 a.m. to support Ian Hamilton to E. Sniping and big guns on our left. Big guns to front 9 a.m. Shells bursting on same ridges as yesterday. Got order to attack ridge to our left (enemies left of position 11 a.m. We marched off 3rd. 12 noon. ... Heavy shelling from Boer gun. 1 shell fell between 2 men of No. 3. Very few burst. Advanced 2.7pm and attacked main position. Heard whistle of pompom. Climbed 1st ridge without getting again under

---

[10] Yes, that's the same family as Princess Diana. The executive summary is that John Churchill, a very rough customer, led the English to victory over the French at Blenheim in 1704 in the War of the Spanish Succession. In gratitude for his achievements, Queen Anne granted him, among other titles, Duke of Marlborough, and funded the building of Blenheim Place at Woodstock. John Churchill had no legitimate son so an act of Parliament, uniquely, allowed the title to pass in the female line. One of John Churchill's daughters married Charles Spencer, third Earl of Sunderland, Diana's forebear, so the Dukes and Duchesses of Marlborough used the family name Spencer until in the 19th century the 5th Duke of Marlborough obtained a royal license to use the name Spencer-Churchill whereupon most family members dropped the Spencer. Winston Churchill was the grandson of the 7th Duke of Marlborough and Captain Churchill was a grandson of the 6th Duke.

Boer fire. Boers' ridge (entrenched) 800 yards from Coldstream. Our own guns firing over our heads all the time. … Lay down rest of day under heavy fire from front and left. At least 10 bullets within 1 foot or so. 1 man in No 4 hit through head quite close."

August 25, 1900: "Lay down for about ½ hour under very hot shell fire (they burst 20 yards in front of the line pieces going all over)."

August 26, 1900: "We advanced 5.20 p.m. and lay down under rifle fire near Monument till dark. 1 man No.5 killed and 1 No.7 wounded. 2 conductors hit and several niggers."

He seems to have spent 1901 until he sailed home on July 22, 1902 running and guarding a supply train. Though clearly the conditions must have been less than ideal or comfortable, he nevertheless had time to go hunting, to scavenge for souvenirs, to dine with friends, *etc.* Two of the amusing entries are:

March 19, 1901: "Good scorpion v. tarantula fight"

May 8, 1901: "White and self dined with male and female Jews–Hotel keepers at Hanover Road, where slept, as trains would not go on owing to Boer scare. Believe we were taken for Boers."

More interesting than diaries are letters to his family, particularly his mother, which he also transcribed and left to the Guards. Here is an excerpt of one dated March 21, 1900, said to be from Glen Station (on Moder):

"Three men including one Trotter and adjutant Lygon, went out foraging 11.30am. saw 7 boers about 7 miles from camp said lets capture them, gave chase boers bolted and took up position on Kopje. C.O. said to adjutant and Trotter 'you are young and active, you go round while we walk up in front' which they did. Boers waited until they fired, then they were all stretched in two minutes. Lygon shot through the heart. Trotter said he lay watching pool of blood getting larger and larger unable to do anything, boers then came down bound them up and carried them to a farm near. We buried Lygon here. Trotter soft bullet which makes all the difference. Shall not want any more handkerchiefs at present. So sorry did not take camera on the march, every oz. tells. Thought should not get films. Am trying hard to get Mauser carbine delightful weapons. Cavalry gone to cut off convoy I hear. Have been buck shooting lately, not got one yet. Hamilton with me got one the other day. Your loving GEORGE"

Here is another from Sunnyside, three miles east of Pretoria, June 19, 1900.

"Got to where we were leaving guards in all important places in Town I was in charge of Grand Hotel and responsible for all streets near. All the prisoners (officers) came round, of course delighted to see us, and told me stories of their surrenders &c. They did not like Winston (he and Marlborough were messing round all morning) as you may imagine."

As for his scavenging and souvenir collection:

July 31: "There was an old grandmother of 97 there who had a most magnificent old Dutch Bible with coloured illustrations all through. Have been trying to get one all the time. Offered her 5d, but she would not look at it said not [£]10 or anything"

He constantly reports his own looting. "We wear Boer hats and bandoliers now" (July 22, 1900).

An interesting note to his mother from Kaffir River Bridge on April 19, 1900 reads in part:

"Had a letter from Gan [grandmother] last mail saying she would give a ball at Northwick to celebrate my return: which I should very much enjoy. Got box of Plasmon biscuits (on which I am writing this) this morning. As far as I can make out from the post mark it was sent on February 8."

The Captain resigned his commission on May 13, 1903 but rejoined his regiment as a captain on September 15, 1914 in the earliest days of World War I (which he always called the Kaiser's War). This time he left no diary or other records, but he won a Military Cross and Croix de Guerre with palm. In 1915, he suffered a serious head wound at Loos[11] when a piece of shrapnel went through his steel helmet, and was in the mortuary when his batman (military servant) noticed his eyelid move. He recovered in 18 months (except for singing noises in his head) and rejoined his company as commander. That batman, Mr Shepherd, became Churchill's chauffeur for life.[12] The helmet was reportedly at Northwick for years but its whereabouts are now unknown.

Churchill's Military Cross citation reads as follows:

"Captain Edward George Spencer-Churchill, G.Gds.

---

[11] Loos was a catastrophe, described by Robert Graves in *Good-Bye to All That*. 20,610 British and Commonwealth casualties with no known grave, not a yard gained or lost. It was the first battle in which the British used chlorine gas (140 tons) of which a significant portion blew back over the British lines. Among the casualties: Rudyard Kipling's son and the brother of Elizabeth II's mother, Mary.

[12] Mr Shepherd had a metal plate in his head (war wound?). He drove Captain Churchill to the train on Tuesdays. Churchill stayed in his flat in London and returned to Blockley on Thursdays when Shepherd picked him up. Shepherd did odd household chores, such as washing dishes. He never went through the front door of the Mansion, always using the service entrance, which is now No. 1 Burlington Court. (This information was obtained by Richard Paice on September 2, 2012, interviewing Mrs June Wadey, who was the wife of the son of the Captain's butler and housekeeper. Mrs Wadey lived over the Stables starting in 1952.)

For conspicuous skill and gallantry while leading a night patrol of eleven men. Shortly after starting an enemy shell wounded one of his party, and he took the wounded man safely back and then he returned and led his patrol forward again through the enemy wire right up to their posts. Whilst lying there a party of some forty of the enemy were seen approaching. He waited until they were within thirty yards and then ordered rapid fire, and emptied his revolver into them. In the confusion that followed he skillfully withdrew his party with only one slight casualty. He inflicted heavy casualties on this enemy party and probably frustrated an intended raid by them."

I speculate that the young, aristocratic junior officer who had a rather good time (all things considered) in the Boer War and carefully preserved all his diaries and letters for posterity almost with a certain smugness, had a different experience in the trenches and saw nothing that he wanted remembered.

Captain Churchill was a remarkable man. It is reported that he refused a courtesy title when his father died and that in the army he refused to be promoted to the rank of major. As a rich Cambridge undergraduate he acquired an x-ray machine purely out of interest before the University got one. He loaned it to the army medical service in the Boer War. As a young man he developed a fascination for Egyptian relics and antiques, and later expanded to Greek and Indian.

The Captain was a sport fisherman and a trip that he took to the United States in 1906 yielded his book *Tarpon Fishing in Mexico and Florida*. First published in 1907, it seems to have become a minor classic. It was republished in 1998 including a limited edition of fifty copies costing $750 each. In these days, original copies of the book in good condition with the sixteen stereo views of tarpon in a pocket in the back carry price tags around $2,600.

I was surprised to find that I actually enjoyed the book even though I have no interest whatsoever in the subject matter. It is dry, good-humored, and written in the present tense as if the Captain is in an adjacent armchair and telling you a story over a drink. Captain Churchill comes across as just what he was, a late-Victorian imperialist gentleman. A product of his class and era, he says things that we would never say today, such as referring to black fishing guides as "darkies". He describes his battles with "jew fish"–very large, wily, tough fish which fight fishermen with a high degree of success and which won his admiration. He explains the name: "These sea perch are so called because they live close to the bottom, open their enormous mouths and suck in everything that comes within reach."[13] I regret noting these things because they prompt his dismissal as a racist and an anti-Semite. Well, yes, but in the nicest possible way. He was an English gentleman from the grandest of families who fought with distinction in two wars. He demonstrated a tremendous sense of duty and compassion throughout his life and these antique, unexamined class prejudices deserve forgiveness in his case; he earned it.

The Captain was a skilled and sensitive real estate developer. He succeeded to the Harrow estates in addition to Northwick and with the development of public transit just before World

---

[13] Churchill p. 28.

War I, he began to subdivide his Harrow holdings. Most of the building began after the war but the first thing he planned in the center of what he called Northwick Circle was the Northwick Park Tennis and Social Club which became quite exclusive but is now, unfortunately, a rather unattractive Masonic office. Fanning out from Northwick Circle are streets with names such as Dovedale, Draycott and Sedgecomb. Nearby are Blockley Road and Paxton Road. Captain Churchill did not build the houses that went up between 1923 and 1932, but he clearly retained some design control in selecting developers–all the houses are mock-Tudor and consistent. This was clearly a well-thought-out, enlightened planned unit development. It is now all in a conservation district so his vision will be largely preserved.

He created the Northwick brickworks after the war to provide employment (the last silk mill had closed in 1901); the bricks were used in the Battersea Power Station. It is reported that Blockley bricks were very high quality and hard-fired. They were purchased and then rejected for the theatre at Stratford because they were too hard and the architect wanted to carve a relief.

In his later years the Captain lived in just one or two rooms in the Mansion, but it remained full of his collections.[14]

The gallery　　　　*The Rotunda*　　　　*The Burlington Room*

Captain Churchill died on June 26, 1964 at the age of eighty-eight of renal failure, having been scalded after falling in his bath in his home on Charles Street in London. His estate was valued at £1,890,710.8.0. The beneficiaries include his employees who received seemingly generous annuities (£200/yr.) or lump sum payments. Many men with titles indicating military rank received specific bequests. He had clearly been very generous in his life and topped up many gifts he had made from 1943 onward. Still, all in all, the will is a lonely and depressing document– the act of an old man scattering his wealth and treasures in a thoughtful, decent way, but dispersing, not consolidating or preserving. He gave his Greek vases and pre-Marcus Aurelius objects to the Ashmolean and British Museums, and before his death negotiated four paintings to the government in lieu of death duties. Everything else was sold, right down to the farm implements. There ensued the famous sales by Christie's.

As to why he ordered the liquidation of so much that he loved, my guess is that he was depressed. He had survived most of his contemporaries and family, lived in one or two rooms of

---

[14] Pictures courtesy of Mrs June Wadey.

the Mansion. He had had a terrible experience in the trenches of World War I. He placed a few choice objects, gave a lot of money to old comrades in arms, and was very nice to the remaining staff. After that it would seem that he just didn't care anymore.

The sales became notorious because the first of them (furniture and furnishings, over three days starting on September 28, 1964) was massively ringed. The dealers in the ring retired every night to the Swan Inn in Moreton-in-Marsh where they divvied up the spoils in a second auction among themselves. As it happened, a newspaper reporter infiltrated the group of dealers and wrote a series of scandalous articles, prompting discussion in Parliament and causing the resignation in disgrace of the then President of the British Antique Dealers Association who led the group.

Where Did the Money Come From to Acquire All this Art and Property?
The Rushouts

Serious disposable income was required to buy and hold a 2,000-acre estate for over three hundred years and to amass two great art collections. The first sight we have of the family fortune starts with John Rushout (John I), a Flemish merchant, whose son, James (James I), acquired Northwick. We do not know much about John I, but what we do know puts the Rushout family in England in context. John I was born in 1593 and arrived in England in 1613, becoming a freeman of the Worshipful Company of Fishmongers in 1631. That does not mean he dealt in fish; joining a livery company, as they are called, was a usual way for an alien who was barred from engaging in retail trade in England to make a place for himself in the City. He received letters of denization, a sort of residency permit, on 21 April 1634 (#7 in the Letters Patent Roll of 10 Charles in the National Archive) in which he is described as a "weaver". His letters read:

> The king to all to whom, etc, greetings. Know you that we have granted from our special grace and our certain knowledge and free volition and by these presents we grant for us, our heirs and successors to the beloved to us John Rushout, weaver, born and originating in parts across the seas, or by whatever other name he may be called, that he, himself, after this during his natural life may be our denizen and subject and that of our heirs and successors, and in all things be held, reputed, etc, as our faithful subject, originating within this our kingdom of England, *etc*. And that he, himself, can and be able to have and exercise all and every kind of actions, suits and quarrels of whatever kind they may be in whatsoever our courts, places and jurisdictions, and use and enjoy the same, and plead and be impleaded in the same, to answer and be answered to, to defend and be defended, in all things, etc, just as any of our faithful subjects originating in our said kingdom of England. And in addition that the same John Rushout can and be able lawfully and without punishment to purchase, receive, take, have, hold, buy and possess lands, tenements, rents, reversions and services and other hereditaments and whatsoever within our said kingdom of England and our other lordships, and to use and enjoy the same, and to give, sell, alienate and bequeath the same to whatever person or persons it may be pleasing for him at his will. And that he, himself, can and be able to hire, have and retain whatever taverns, shops or houses for a term of one year or more years fully, freely, quietly, wholly and peacefully, just as any of our subjects born within our said kingdom of England. And that it may be and will be lawful for any of our subjects to bequeath to the aforesaid John Rushout and his assigns whatsoever taverns, shops or houses for the term of one year or more years without any forfeiture or penalty whatsoever to be incurred by this occasion. And also that the same John Rushout can have and possess all and every kind of liberties, franchises and privileges of this our kingdom freely, quietly, wholly and peacefully and use and enjoy the same as our faithful subject born within our said kingdom of England without disturbance, impediment, molestation, vexation, charge or

accusation from us, our heirs and successors or any others whatsoever, any statute, act, ordinance or provision formerly issued, made, ordained or provided to the contrary thereof or any other thing, cause or matter whatsoever not withstanding.

Provided always that the same John Rushout does liege homage to us and pay and contribute 'lott and scott', just as our other subjects do and contribute, as is just. And that the same John Rushout is held and may be obedient to all and singular the ordinances, acts, statutes and proclamations of this our kingdom of England both issued and to be issued in the future according to the form of the statute recently issued and provided in this regard. Provided also always that, if the aforesaid John Rushout will practice trade or the art of merchandise as a merchant at any time in the future and bring in or cause to be imported goods

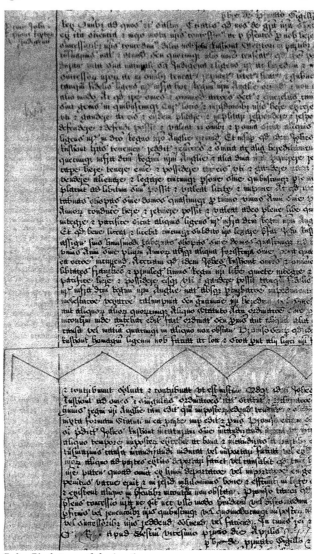

John I's letters of denization

and merchandise from foreign parts and from across the seas, or make or will cause them to be exported outside our kingdom to foreign parts, then our letters patent as regards all issues from this exporting or importing will be completely void and in the residue will nevertheless stand and be good and effectual in law, anything in the present to the contrary not withstanding. Provided nevertheless that this, our present grant, may not be nor in any way will be a prejudice or source of damage to our profits or revenues, etc, to be handed over, paid or made to us, our heirs or successors in the future. In testimony of which matter, *etc*. Witnessed by the king at Westminster on the twenty first day of April. By writ of privy seal.

(Translated by Simon Neal)

John Rushout's first wife, Abigail.[15]

At some point John Rushout married the daughter of Joas Godschalck. Joas was said to be born in Nieukerck in Flanders, and was a member of a large and economically successful clan of Flemish wool merchants who spelled the name variously, including "Godschall". Joas received letters of denization on October 25, 1605 (Joas also tried to receive naturalization, the equivalent of citizenship, but failed to do so in the House of Lords on 24 March 1623). The registers of the Dutch Church Austin Friars contain baptisms of John's children starting in 1627. John became a deacon of that church in 1632 and an elder in 1641. He was later associated with St. Dionis Back-Church where his son John was buried in 1648.[16] As a "merchant stranger" John Rushout was noted in the tax records as one of the wealthiest inhabitants of Langbourne Ward in 1640. He "took no ascertainable part in the Civil War".[17]

---

[15] Abigail was born in 1606 and the painting says the sitter was in her 29th year in 1631, so there is an inconsistency, but dates on pictures can be wrong. And then there's the matter of the name itself–see footnote 19.

[16] N. Hardy, "'Faith's Victory over Nature'–Sermon Preached at the Funeral of Master John Rushout." This was printed in 1658, ten years after the death of the boy and five years after the death of the father who, I suspect, prepaid for the publication and left Hardy £30 in his will. (PROB 11/236 in the National Archive). There are no useful family references in the sermon.

[17] *The History of Parliament: The House of Commons, 1660-1690*, B.D. Henning, ed. (HMSO), p. 357.

This is a portrait of John Rushout and his family, which I think was painted in about 1643.[18] John is on the left; next is his son John, John II, who died in 1648 (Gregorian) after a fall from a horse. His first wife[19] holds daughter Ann on her lap; then come Katherine and Abigail. Dating the picture is easy. The mother died May 23, 1644 and her daughter Ann was born October 10, 1641. The baby looks to be about 18-24 months old so that must be Ann. The setting of the portrait does not relate to any property that John Rushout is known to have owned.

There is an interesting artifact of the dead boy. He was sent to a Latin school in Amsterdam, where he left this autograph in his teacher's "friends book" in 1645:

---

[18] The painting is about 6' x 10' and has been attributed to Cornelius Johnson (died 1661) and also to Thomas de Critz (died 1653). None of the family pictures were sold in the famous Northwick sale of 1859, probably because they were treated as heirlooms (property which goes with the house on succession). The claim for Johnson appears in an article on Cornelius Jansen in *Anecdotes of Painting in England* by Horace Walpole based on the notes of George Vertue with additions by James Dallaway, p. 213, fn. 4 (1828). Whether the same note is in the original 1762 edition I do not know but the note says that Johnson (original name Jansen or Janssens) in 1636 lived with a Flemish merchant named Arnold Braems and painted the Rushout family, then of Maylands in Essex, and that the picture is "Now at Northwick, Worcestershire." It sounds plausible as Johnson also painted a very similar large picture of the Capel family in about 1641 which is in the National Portrait Gallery in London and John Rushout was a Flemish merchant. The painting was sold in the Churchill auction (attributed to de Critz) in 1965 but I have not been able to locate it.

[19] The wife's name is a bit of a mystery. Most records say her name was Ann. Joas Godschalck's will dated July 20, 1652 (WRO Box 43A) refers to his "late daughter Anne, wife of John Rushout" but John Rushout's will repeatedly says it was Abigail. James Rushout, her son, wrote a family genealogy in which he gives her name as Abigail and *The Reiester Book of Saynte De'Nis*, the family church (St. Dionis Backchurch) records the burial of Abigail Rushout, wife of John Rushout, on May 28, 1644. I labeled the picture "Abigail" though the museum that owns it calls her Ann. The sitter's costume is about 1625; it seems like a trophy portrait of a young bride and the long nose is distinctive.

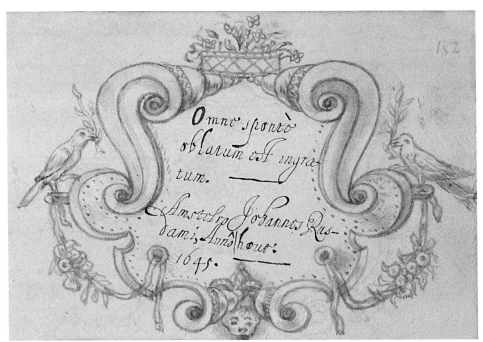

John Rushout's autograph; the 1645 equivalent of signing your teacher's yearbook.

Below, this lovely emblazoned pedigree for John Rushout in the Worcestershire County Records Office is said to have been made in 1652 tracing his line back to "Thieband Rushaut" in 1300; the parchment is about as long as your arm.

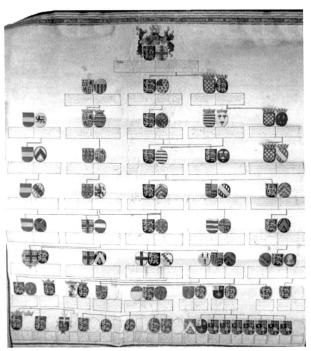

It includes what were claimed as the Rushout arms of two gold lions passant (walking) guardant (looking out at you). It's the one on the left.[20]

The Rushout pedigree

---

[20] I have not investigated (heraldry is not an amateur's game) and at best it would tell me something about medieval France which is not my thing. Knowing that someone's grandfather was a duke is terribly important to a psychiatrist, an anthropologist or a relative but probably of secondary interest in this chronicle.

In the 16th and 17th centuries it was normal for people clawing their way into the landed gentry to have these remarkable genealogies created; who knows if even the sponsor believed them. One Tudor magnate, Arthur Heveningham, had his family traced back to one "Arphaxad", a knight who "watched Christ's sepulcher". For what it is worth, the claim is made for Rushout that among his ancestors was grand master of horse for Louis XI (r. 1461-83). The Rushouts became progressively grand in their pretensions as years went by. It seems that a gold lion passant, guardant is found in the arms of the earliest kings of France before the Norman Conquest and when Henry II, who used two lions, married Eleanor of Acquitane, he added one more for a total of three. Allegedly the Rushout family then changed their family motto to "Par Ternis Suppar," which translates loosely "A pair more than a match for three" or, perhaps, "Two of greater antiquity than three." They also promoted an alleged connection between the name "Rushout" and the name "Roualt" or "Ronalt" which features in the names of the first three kings of France. H. Sydney Grazebrook reviewed these claims in *Heraldry of Worcestershire*, London, 1873, and found them, to put it charitably, unproven.

The facts are that there was a Ruysschout family living near Izegem (which is west of Brussels) in the 1380s and John I's great-grandfather lived in Izegem in the mid-1500s. The family can be traced in Flanders until John I left for London, followed a few years later by his sister Josina (Joyce).[21] Thus the claimed pedigree is pure rubbish and John I knew it. His heirs had to have known as well.

---

[21] I am indebted to Daan de Clercq for sharing his extraordinary genealogy of the Rushouts.

A DIGRESSION: THE RUSHOUTS AND THE TRADING COMPANIES[22]

Since there is so little known about John I, I digress into a short history of 17th-century English commerce in which I attempt to link three known facts and grow them into a picture. Those facts are: (1) John Rushout and his father-in-law, Joas Godschalck, were among a rising class of merchant adventurers operating in England in the second quarter of the 17th century; (2) John's son James became a Baronet at the Restoration in 1661 at the age of 17, ten years after John's death, and (3) James went on to be appointed the Crown's ambassador to Constantinople and thus in substance the ambassador of The Governor and Company of Merchants of England Trading into the Levant (a/k/a the Levant Company) in 1697. It is a long stretch with not much to go on.

The first rule in sleuthing is to follow the money. If you will indulge me for about five pages, you will have a glimmer of how to make a pile in 17th-century England. Or you can skip this section. In the first half of the 16th century, England did well exporting semi-finished heavy broadcloth wool piece goods into northern Europe. The trade was controlled by the Company of Merchant Adventurers, a legal entity with a charter granting monopolies, which the Tudors found lucrative and therefore sponsored. A symbiotic relationship developed in which the sovereign protected the merchants' monopolies in exchange for a piece of the action and, in addition, the merchants could be tapped for significant loans to the Crown (which was always short of the necessary). The Merchant Adventurers were literally a specific group of what we would now call venture capitalists. I use the term with capitals to describe this investor class and to distinguish them from merchant traders who dealt in goods as wholesalers and retailers. Merchant Adventurers dealt in title to goods and financed their acquisition but never dirtied their hands.

Then, starting about 1550, the northern European textile market began to stagnate, heading into a collapse by 1640 as a drive for cheaper goods shifted centers of production. The demand for heavy wool was pushed down by soaring imports of silk from the near and then far east. To the extent that the trade route was through Holland, the Merchant Adventurers got a piece of the action but when direct shipment from Persia and Asia began, the Merchant Adventurers were hurt. The trade was also adversely affected by periodic wars. Depending on who England was at war with, trade either was stopped (*e.g.* English trade to the Netherlands stopped in 1562 and 1564) or the trading vessels of the warring nations were mutually plundered with governmental sanction under letters of marque for reprisal. Possibly because they held monopolies in a lucrative short-route trade into Northern Europe, which gave them quick turnover and little transit risk, the Merchant Adventurers were not quick to adapt. They largely ignored the developing markets in Spain, the East Indies and in the Mediterranean (Venice and Turkey). These new markets were developed by more responsive, innovative men whose backgrounds were no different from those of the Merchant Adventurers but who, not being members of the protected club, were more aggressive and imaginative. The Turkey Company,

---

[22] This section relies extensively on *Merchants and Revolution*, Robert Brenner, Verso, 2003.

consisting of twenty-eight merchants (eight of them London aldermen, three MP's[23]), received a Crown Patent (a royal license) in 1581. When that patent lapsed, the Levant Company (the Levant was the eastern Mediterranean from Greece to Egypt) was chartered with fifty-three members. That membership expanded to five hundred in the early 17th century but included largely the same group of wealthy men with commercial and family connections—at one point forty to fifty percent of the members were related by blood or through marriage.

Levant Company members in turn were preeminent in the Governor and Company of Merchants of London Trading into the East Indies (a/k/a the East India Company) founded in 1600 in part because both companies were focused on the importation of spices. In the 1630s the directors of the two companies substantially over-lapped. These men were at the top of London's commercial establishment and populated the social and political elite, taking over from, but not extinguishing, the Merchant Adventurers who remained as the diminishing old money.

The Levant Company members of the East India Company who owned big ships, which were the key to the trade, began to venture into the Far East following the Portuguese and the Dutch. They started their East India venture on a small scale in 1601—one or two highly speculative exploratory voyages. The first voyage was of four ships returning in two years. The objective was always to obtain luxury goods in Asia which could be distributed in, and from, England at great profit. There was no real market for the usual English goods in Asia so they left England with gold and silver and came back with spices and silk, a specie imbalance which eventually created economic and political problems. To secure goods in Asia, they established permanent trading outposts manned by men called factors (*i.e.,* do-ers). Their outpost warehouses were thus called factories but nothing was made there. Instead the factor would spend a year assembling goods from local suppliers to fill Company-owned ships, which shuttled back and forth. The capital of these trading companies was largely tied up in ships and the fitting out of ships. Between 1600 and 1620 the East India Company had built seventy-six ships in its two shipyards on the Thames (thus becoming one of the largest employers in the London area) and set up a dozen trading stations in Asia. Between 1601 and 1612 the investors participated voyage-by-voyage; the first actual joint stock company was formed in 1613 under a ten-year charter. Originally the aristocracy was not welcome to invest but after 1609 as Parliament became more and more obstreperous about the granting of exclusive trading privileges, the advantages of having friends at court became more obvious even though the aristocracy were less than dependable in meeting their financial obligations. Foreigners, particularly Dutch merchants, who were excluded from membership in the Dutch East India Company, the VOC, were major investors. Actually in the 1620s the East India Company partnered for a while with the VOC.

You could not become a member of one of these elite companies unless you were a "mere merchant", a rather misleading term meaning that you were an importer/exporter or wholesaler, not a shopkeeper, warehouseman, manufacturer or sea captain (captains were allowed to do a little import/export business on the side and tended to sell at retail). You were indeed drummed out of the Company if you lapsed into the lower ranks of the merchant trade, a rule perhaps created to make sure that you could not be an interloper (*i.e.* someone trading in violation of a Company monopoly) while being a Company member.

---

[23] Broken down by trading background, nine were investors in the Muscovy Company, ten were in the Spanish Company, eight were in both companies and one was in neither.

Interloping was a big issue for the privileged trading companies and it became more and more prevalent in the first half of the 17th century in part because Charles I became a silent partner of some of the interlopers. Charles I even had his own privateering vessel doing coastal raiding in the Red Sea, which created problems for the East India Company.

The first quarter of the 17th century saw James I and Charles I selling trading privileges to the merchants to raise revenue and Parliament increasingly attacking those same privileges. Through the reign of King James I, the merchants on the whole were royalists and suspicious of Parliament. Yet the merchant adventurer class was quite political because unlike the landed classes who could collect their rents no matter who was in power, the adventurers needed their government-protected privileges.

It is ironic, therefore, that Charles I really alienated the merchant adventurers through corruption and a pattern of side-deals granting privileges and honors. Charles' basic problem was that he was a flake–he could never keep a deal either economically or politically. A product of the Elizabethan fundamentally magic-oriented mindset, Charles honestly believed that he was a divine right king who could at any moment do as he wished, no matter what he had said or promised earlier. Eventually that trait cost him his head because he would make political deals with Parliament to clean up his royal act, then go right out and engage in the same high-handed behavior that caused the first phase of the Civil War. He wouldn't stay bought–often a fatal trait.

Charles I, bribed by the gift of a secret £10,000 interest in the venture, licensed a company to trade in all areas of the East not previously exploited by the East India Company–areas thought of as under-exploited or under-settled and under-fortified. The new company was organized in 1635 by William Courteen (also spelled Courten), an Anglo-Dutch trader, Crown lender and "one of London's great merchant princes". The Courteen company, among other things, attempted to establish a settlement in Assada, off the coast of Madagascar and sent out one hundred forty colonists. When Courteen died, his son, also named William, reorganized the company in 1637 and competed head-to-head with the East India Company, a competition ruinous to both parties. By 1642, William Courteen was bankrupt and fled to the Continent leaving control of his company in the hands of his partners, including Joas Godschalck and John Rushout. John Rushout and his father-in-law took over some of Courteen's estates, including the manor of Wyre Piddle, six miles east of Evesham.

Why Godschalck and Rushout were in London with the rest of these Dutch traders and whether they were ever really part of the Flemish textile trade is unknown to me, but it is worth noting that exports of the Flemish cloth industry fell 50% in the 17th century–so even if they were originally in that trade, they might have been looking for greener pastures or might have been flight capitalists. More generally, Philip II of Catholic Spain had inherited the Low Countries, including Flanders, and on the theory that what was bad for Spain was good for England, Elizabeth I invited Flemish merchants and textile workers–mainly Protestants–to England.

Letters of denization which Godschalck and Rushout obtained were a sort of residency permit in the form of letters patent issued by the Crown in its discretion. It was less than full citizenship but, importantly, gave the alien the right to buy and sell real property and pass it by will. The grants were all conditional and the restrictions could vary. In the case of an alien merchant who would otherwise have to pay full duty on his imports and exports, the Crown was not usually disposed to forgo that revenue so their letters were often conditioned on the merchants continuing to pay customs as aliens. The other route to security was to receive letters of naturalization, which took an act of Parliament and made one unconditionally a full citizen. John Rushout tried for that in 1651 but he got no further than the second of three required "readings" in Parliament on May 20, 1651.

Rushout's letters of denization are quite clear that

> "if the aforesaid John Rushout will practice trade or the art of merchandise as a merchant at any time in the future and bring in or cause to be imported goods and merchandise from foreign parts and from across the seas, or make or will cause them to be exported outside our kingdom to foreign parts, then our letters patent as regards all issues from this exporting or importing will be completely void and in the residue will nevertheless stand and be good and effectual in law, anything in the present to the contrary notwithstanding."

This meant that on trade related issues, he could not sue or defend in the King's courts. That was a greater peril than most of these sorts of grants imposed. Letters normally said that if the patentee traded, he was taxed as an alien. Rushout's tax exposure was broader as well. His letters conclude: "Provided nevertheless that this, our present grant, may not be nor in any way will be a prejudice or source of damage to our profits or revenues, *etc.*, to be handed over, paid or made to us, our heirs or successors in the future."

All this suggests to me that Rushout did not engage in trade as a "mere merchant" but was instead a merchant adventurer or, more likely, a moneylender. An inventory made on Rushout's death in 1653 totaled £28,920 including £23,058 of "debts good and hopeful" and nothing that looks like a serious inventory of goods.

There were communities of foreign businessmen resident in England throughout much of the 16th and 17th centuries (*viz.*: the Germans in the "Steelyard", the London warehouse/residential section where they traded). The new merchants had close connections, particularly in Holland, which extended to connections by marriage. The thirteen-member Assada syndicate included six "Dutchmen" and the Commonwealth tried very hard to establish a sort of commercial union with the United Provinces using these Dutchmen as go-betweens. These new men formed part of a new, second tier elite. Their progress proceeded apace with the decline of the East India Company, which came on hard times and almost dissolved in the middle of the 17th century after a disastrous voyage to the east.

Charles I (and especially his mentor, the fundamentally corrupt and corrupting Duke of Buckingham[24]) squeezed the merchants too hard and in particular began to assert direct control over trade with the West Indies and Virginia. The merchants finally tipped momentarily to the side of Parliament in 1626 and supported the impeachment of Buckingham. Charles and

---

[24] The Duke, George Villiers, captivated both James I and Charles I and was probably the lover of James I. He rose to the dukedom and became the dispenser of royal patronage, honors, etc. He engaged in unsavory diplomatic intrigues, led an army with disastrous results and was finally assassinated by one of his lieutenants. His son was a real pill as well and served as a sidekick to Charles II in his frolics.

Parliament were in a stand-off. Charles called for a £100,000 loan from his usual sources in the City, which was not forthcoming so he imposed a "forced loan" on them. That tore it. True, the merchants played both sides and in the closing years of the 1620s some of them made considerable loans to Charles but basically the second tier merchants were content to have their resistance to Charles' levies on their imports and profits included in the broader constitutional grievances of Charles' abuse of his privileges.

To illustrate how bad it got, Charles seized currants (a major source of income for the Levant Company) because the Company members would not pay a duty surcharge he imposed. Fourteen members of the Levant Company broke into the government warehouse to retrieve their goods. This was no London rabble–it is as if a bunch of Wall Street executives were engaging in commercial civil disobedience at the felony level.

Yet the merchants never broke cleanly with the Crown; the top social tier in particular, the Merchant Adventurers, had its own reasons for trying to support Charles. The rest of them were probably too smart to put all their political eggs in one basket but clearly the critical mass tipped and their commercial concerns were taken up in the broader movement to curb the king's arbitrary exercise of his prerogatives.

The pendulum partially swung back in the 1640s as the merchant elite were frightened by the emerging radicalism in Parliament which was attacking not only royal prerogatives but also bent on "reforming" the City and re-writing its constitution.[25] The City aldermanic court was heavily populated by merchant adventurers and had been through most of the century; radical change was not in its interest. The new men included significant numbers of Parliament supporters but the old guard in the elite companies came down by a heavy preponderance on the royal side.

The new men, particularly the East Indian interlopers with whom Rushout was associated, tended to be on the parliamentary side along with the new traders into America and Africa. I have not gone into the records to see if Rushout signed any of the petitions that circulated through the City and Parliament on both sides in the 1640s or invested in the Additional Sea Adventure to Ireland (a private army and fleet to conquer the place once and for all [it failed]) or the groups that raised money to support Parliament in the war but somehow I doubt that he would have done anything that visible.

---

[25] The Puritan Parliament actually banned the import of currants (the mainstay of Levant Company trading) into England on the ground that they were a useless product draining money out of England. The merchant traders entered politics to protect themselves. For example, in addition to John Rushout and his father-in-law, there were eleven members of the Assada interlopers led by Thomas Andrews. Two of them, Andrews and John Fowke, were among the one hundred thirty member court that tried Charles I. Another, Stephen Estwicke, was a judge in the lower level treason trials. (Brenner p. 548) Andrews and Estwicke were also members of the High Court of Justice created in 1650 to root out supporters of the King. The inroads that the new merchant interlopers made in the 1640s were extraordinary. When the East India Company fell on hard times, sixteen of the new men, including Thomas Andrews, became directors of the Second General Voyage (See British Library India House Office, East India Company Court Minutes vol. B/24, pp. 7-10, 1-8 Sept 1647). The first Lord Mayor of London during the Commonwealth was this same Thomas Andrews, Rushout's partner. Andrews and Estwicke were the leaders of a petition to recall the Rump (the Parliamentarians who remained when the royalists and centrists were forced out; the Rump tried Charles I). Cromwell eventually veered to the right to resist some of the more radical impulses of his supporters including Andrews and Estwicke who were swept from office giving new life to the old guard merchants who had royalist tendencies. The business of England being business, no matter who was in power, most of the new men gradually maneuvered back into positions of individual influence but from 1653, the power remained with the more conservative members of the merchant trader community.

In 1650, the Commonwealth needed both revenue and a general expansion of trade. Notwithstanding the royalist leanings of the East India Company, the Commonwealth in effect put it back in business and forced an amalgamation of all the trading companies including Rushout's Assada venture into a single joint stock company which was effectively led by the new merchants, not the old guard. No Rushout was ever a Governor of the East India Company and none ever served as a member of its board of directors called the Court of Committees. The stock ledgers before 1675 are gone so we do not know if John was ever a "Proprietor", as the shareholders were called. However, the accounting of the estate of John's mother-in-law, Anne Godschalck, dated February 8, 1655 (1656) acknowledges a receipt of £409.04.04 from the East India Company and "The Account of the Mortuary House of Mrs. Anne Godschalck draws a receipt on April 28, 1654 of £162.10 from the East India Company. (Her estate paid out £1192.04.9 and received £1565.04.7, so while she was not poor, clearly her son-in-law John was the successful one.)

JAMES RUSHOUT, 1ST BARONET

John I's first wife, Abigail, died May 23, 1644, possibly consequent on the birth of their son James who was born March 24, 1643.[26] John re-married to Elizabeth Finnet Godschalck, the widow of his first wife's brother.[27] John I died in 1653. James I was his nine-year old heir, John's first son to survive infancy, a prior son (also John) having died in a fall from his horse in 1648.[28]

The first report we have of James (other than his father's will dated September 23, 1653) is that he was created a Baronet on June 17, 1661, about a year after Charles II was returned to the throne. A Baronetcy was a status created and sold by King James I for about £1,000 a pop. It was not a knighthood though the titleholder was called 'Sir'. It was inheritable in the male line. About 3,500 of these titles were sold, many in the 17th century. Charles II needed to replenish the royal coffers so he sold a lot and I assume James Rushout, a young, wealthy man hoping for status, was a purchaser.[29]

James' next promotion was to become MP for Evesham in May 1670, presumably based on his late father's estates in the area.

James married Alice Pitt sometime after October 15, 1668, which is the date of a letter to him from his future mother-in-law discussing competitive bids for her daughter's hand. Apparently the would-be bride's grandfather and uncle thought there was a better deal out there

---

[26] James I is said to have been born March 22, 1643 but that is Julian dating. In Gregorian dating that would be March 24, 1644, or about two months before his mother's death.

Until 1752, England used the Julian calendar under which the New Year began on March 25th so in this example the date March 24, 1646 would be March 24, 1647 in the Gregorian calendar. This is further complicated because some relevant dates are quoted as regnal years which start on the date of ascension (not coronation). So Henry VII became king on August 22, 1485 which meant that his first regnal year (styled conventionally as 1 Henry VII) began August 22, 1485 and ended August 21, 1486. When you overlap regnal and Julian dates you get a headache which can further be complicated by orthographic issues. For example, James Rushout wrote in his own hand that he signed a power of attorney "this twelfth day of March 1687 and in the fourth year of the reign of our Sovereign Lord King James the 2nd over England etc." The first problem was that the 8 in 1687 was scripted almost as an infinity sign or an 'S' lying on its side sort of like ~. I first read that as a poorly-scribed 9, which upon reflection made no sense because James II was long gone by then. To be sure that 8 was right, I tried to correlate the regnal dates. Charles II died on February 6, 1684 (Julian) so 1 James II goes from February 6, 1684 to February 5, 1685 which means that IV James II had to begin on February 5, 1687 and end on February 5, 1688. So March 12, 1687 is right–except of course we would call that March 12, 1688 (Gregorian). Thank God none of the relevant dates were in early September 1752 because to convert to the Gregorian system which makes a leap year adjustment to true-up every four years and to clear out accumulated differences, in 1752 in England September 2nd was followed by September 14th. The missing eleven days and general dissatisfaction with the calendar reform became a political issue of some import but that's a story for another day. In this text, except as noted, all dates up to 1752 are Julian.

[27] This is absolutely typical of this class in this period. Family and business were bonded. The best illustration is in a long article by Mary Edmond in the Proceedings of the Walpole Society, Vol. 47 called "Limners and Picturemakers" in which she traces the repeated connections by blood and marriage among the miniaturists and large scale portrait painters working in London in the 16th and 17th centuries.

[28] John Rushout I had eight children by his first wife, née Ann/Abigail Godschalck. Justus Rushout died at birth on February 23 1626 (Julian). John was born on April 29, 1629 and died in a fall from a horse on March 18, 1647 (Julian). James died at birth on July 5, 1632. Abigail was born June 23, 1634 and died April 3, 1678. Catherine (sometimes spelled with a 'K') was born on November 25, 1631. Anne was born on October 10, 1641. William was born on September 30, 1642 and died the following February 11th and another James was born on March 24, 1643 (Julian).

[29] The palm of a severed hand on his arms is the symbol of a Baronet. I am indebted to John Adye for that clue.

but the grandfather "did bring the business to be examined by a great person" and James got the nod.

The bride, Alice Pitt, was the daughter and heir of Edward Pitt of Harrow-on-the-Hill, Middlesex, thus beginning a long family relationship with Harrow and its famous school, a subject to which we will return later.

James was rich. His father's will (abstracted by James in his own hand) made specific bequests totaling £16,501 to others before leaving the residue to James who also would have received all the real estate outside the will. An inventory of the father's estate showed liquid receivables of £28,920.0.9. In 1692, James prepared "An Account of £30,000 (which was my Estate in Money when I married) How layed out or disposed of in land or at interest stated May 30, 1692." Between buying Northwick and four other properties in Blockley he had spent £17,295.5. That with other land he bought in other counties got him to £29,531.5. He had a net £750 lent at interest which gave him assets of £35,281 from which he deducted £3600 on account of a sale and reached a total of £31,681.5. He concludes: "Thus, I have advanced since I married £1681.5". This seems to be pure cash accounting because he notes, among other things, that he spent £5,000 "in building at Northwick". James' balance sheets for 1670 and 1674 list a "capital" of over £45,000 and that is just cash and financial assets, not real estate, but by itself was a considerable sum in a period when £7-10,000 was a sufficient bribe for a king. The National Archives' currency calculator suggests a conversion multiplier of 80 for a pound in 1680.

James' account book for the period April 1, 1665 through September 27, 1678 survives.[30] It is meticulous but hard to understand because, for instance, there are long lists of cash debits but no credits–so it seems the clerk used the word "debit" to mean a cash transfer in or out. There are many entries called "profit and loss", which seem to be the cash note of a transaction in a balance sheet.

The ledger is the third in a series but is the only known survivor. It provides an insight into how James' affairs were conducted and is illustrative of the development of banking in the later 17th century. James born on March 22, 1644 (Gregorian) and his father died on October 28, 1653, when he was nine years old. Nothing survives which would indicate how his affairs were

---

[30] I own the original but a copy can be found in microfilm form in the Guildhall Library. The ledger is a large, pre-ruled bound volume (12 x 17 inches; 43 x 29 cm) containing about one hundred pages of which the first forty-eight are filled on both sides with very small but relatively clear handwriting. It simply notes day-by-day cash expenditures and receipts mixing recoveries of capital by way of repayments of loans with expenditures for delivery of letters but the bulk of it reflects interest payments on loans and rent payments. On the left hand side of each page beside each entry there are references to journals that have not survived. A typical reference would be 25/31, which may be a reference to a page in another volume setting forth the details of the transaction in question so that the disbursements and recovery of principal on loans or rent received from a tenant would have its own page in the designated book. There is no discernable pattern in the references and I infer that over the twelve or so years in question, as one book got filled up, they moved on to another. The entries seem to be made in the same hand and are occasionally dated "London" which suggests that Sir James' man of business, William Jarrett, had an office there with a clerk or it may be Jarrett's own hand. There is consistently an umlaut over the "y" which suggests that the scrivener was Continental. Sir James did have balance sheets prepared in the same hand, suggesting some attempt at double-entry bookkeeping. Some entries stylize the receipt as being "debits to the capital of Sir James" (e.g., receipts of inheritance) but there is no such note when loan proceeds are repaid and even though this is a cash ledger, there are no notations of loans being advanced–just payments. There are many entries for large sums such as £100 or £200 being paid to William Jarrett with no further accounting as to what Jarrett did with the money but typically in this period and indeed well into the 19th century, a "man of business" (which is what Jarrett was) would have paid all of the household accounts.

managed during his minority, but his father's brother William was an executor of the father's will and the executors were to administer James' inheritance until James was twenty-one–so maybe William purchased James' baronetcy when James was sixteen years old. The cash ledger that has survived begins in April 1665 when James was twenty-one.

The ledger shows that at least until 1675, James was a moneylender, not a trader, and was only a venture capitalist in a very small way. He did not directly manage his money himself. He employed a man named William Jarrett, who is an heir under his father's will, as his "man of business" to make some loans and pay his bills but to a significant extent James participated in the nascent money market using the services early practitioners of what became banking.[31]

In the late 16th and early 17th centuries there was a trade known as a scrivener. The scriveners not only copied documents, they also prepared them and the line between an attorney and a scrivener was unclear at least in the field of preparing legal documentation.

Scriveners began to manage their clients' affairs, collecting rents and managing their real property, and then branched into money-broking in which for a small fee, they would put together lenders and borrowers and administer the loans. Perhaps in part because of the dangers of moving money around (it was all coins–there was no paper money), the scriveners began to hold their clients' money for them in the form of non-interest bearing deposits while awaiting opportunities to lend them for the account of the of the client. Because the economy was agriculture-based, there were slow seasons for lending and the scriveners began to lend their clients' deposits short-term for the scriveners' own account. When the scriveners acted as brokers they had no responsibility for repaying the loan but when they were lending deposits, they did so at their own risk. Because it was a lucrative business, the scriveners began to make money and began to lend their own considerable capital as well.

Among the earliest of these scrivener proto-bankers was a partnership consisting of James Morris and Robert Clayton. Rushout's cash ledger contains myriad transactions in which he has money on deposit with James Morris and Robert Clayton. By April 1672, the firm is identified as Robert Clayton and Company. In some cases it is clear that the firm had brokered loans for James but in other cases it appears that James was lending to the firm at interest.

James also dealt with the other group of proto-bankers, the goldsmiths, who by the nature of their trade were used to handling specie and became moneychangers and lenders. James' cash ledger is full of loans to John East, a goldsmith with premises at the Sun in the Strand and later to East and his partner Theodore Cock. James also made at least one loan in 1668 to John Portman, a Lombard Street goldsmith.

The loans that James made were huge. The National Archives' web site suggests that a pound in 1670 would be the equivalent of £83.05 in 2005 and that £1:4:1 would buy seventeen days of a craftsman's wages in the building trades in 1670. James' cash ledger has dozens of loans of one thousand to two thousand pounds–call it £85,000-£170,000 today. Morris and Clayton were among the originators of the real property mortgage as a form of security, so that is probably why after about 1670 James can be seen to be making secured loans including one for

---

[31] The Bank of England was first organized in 1694 as a private bank (and so remained until 1946).

£1,700 to William Penn, the founder of Philadelphia, secured by a mortgage on Warminghurst, Penn's home which became and remains a sort of Quaker shrine.

It is hard to track James' travels. On August 29, 1671, the ledger shows a credit of £7.15.0 to rent "arrears left by Sir James when he went away." On October 2 and 5, 1671 there are small charges for letters sent to and from "Montpelier". On January 18, 1672 (Gregorian) £200 was sent to "Montpelier". Also recorded on September 8, 1674, was £150 "to Sir James at his departure to France", but Lady Rushout collected £100 in cash in England in September 1674 and £50 in cash in England on December 21, 1674, so she was not with him. She also drew £50 on January 29, February 27 and April 12 of 1675, with James not receiving money "payed in his hands" until May 14, 1675, when he too got £50. Clearly James went at least once more in 1678/9.

We can see in the cash ledger the development of what may be commercial transactions. In 1669 through 1670 there are a series of relatively small transactions in currencies I cannot identify but may have been florins. At any rate they're listed in the currency with an exchange rate and posted in pounds. They tend to be round numbers, such as thirty pounds and later one or two hundred pounds. These foreign exchange transactions occurred mainly between 1671 and 1676.[32]

I doubt these transfers are commercial transactions but I am not sure how to read the entries. It seems that they represent a bill (in modern parlance a "draft", which is sort of an order like a check) in an odd amount of foreign currency. For example, entries reproduced below appear to say "23 Feb 1672 [Gregorian] to M.ᵉ DuLivid upon two bills remitted for Paris at 52 5/8 [symbol] paid as £200:0:0" or, earlier on "18 Jan 1672 to Jerommol [?] Mirando a bill of

---

[32] With Gregorian dates, they appear as follows:

Date	Place	Amount
August 3, 1671	Lyon	£200
August 25, 1671	Bloys	£253:9:0
October 20, 1671	Lyon	£200
November 7, 1671	Lyon	£100
December 4, 1671	Lyon	£200
January 18, 1672	Montpelier	£200
February 23, 1672	Paris	£200
March 15, 1672	Lyon	£200
May ___, 1672	Lyon	£200
June 6, 1672		£152:17:0
July 2, 1672	Paris "inter alia for Mᵉ Morton"	£150
August 20, 1672		£300
January 10, 1673	Lyon "inter alia for Mᵉ Morton"	£100
February 15, 1673	Lyon	£200
April 28, 1673		£150
June 2, 1673		£200
August 15, 1673	Lyon	£150
October 7, 1673	Paris	£100
December 20, 1673	Paris	£100
January 8, 1674	Paris	£150
February 5, 1674	Lyon	£100
February 23, 1674	Lyon	£100
February 13, 1675	Legorn	£90
February 19, 1675	Legorn	£110:7:9
March 24, 1675	Legorn	£140
April 27, 1675	Rome	£100
May 22, 1675	Lyon	£77:10:00
June 19, 1675	Bologna	£100
June 26, 1675	Paris	£45
December 1675	Amsterdam	£1500 (two transactions)
December 1675	Antwerp	£1000 (two transactions)

[symbol] 914:17// a 52 ½ [symbol]-2 [symbol] in Montpelier [sic] paid as £200:0:0." Do those indicate that James bought something in France (assuming these were livres) in an odd amount and the Seller's banker drew on James' banker for that amount, which James' banker posted in pounds?

But it makes more sense that James drew the livres equivalent of £200 on a French correspondent of his London banker and settled the exchange rate locally.[33]

The ledger is a fascinating thing: pages and pages of meticulous transcription without so much as a stray inkblot. My son describes it as looking and feeling like a magician's spellbook.

James Rushout's cash book

---

[33] For the January 18, 1672 exchange dealing of Montpelier mentioned, the symbol looking like 'w' is the shorthand of French écu of three livres tournois, the second symbol is 'd' representing penny, and the third symbol is the shorthand of 'usance', which was the fixed length of time before the payment. Hence, the entry on January 18, 1672 can be read as a bill of 914 écu, 17 sous at a rate of 52½ English pence for one écu of double usance in Montpelier. The usance period was set by custom for each destination. For example, in the second half of the 17th century, the usance between London and Paris is one month after the date of the bill. Hence, "2/double usance" means two months. The French écu was first introduced as gold coin in the mid-13th century. In the 17th century 'écu' generally referred to a large silver coin initially worth three livres tournois. The French money-of-account at the time was 1 livres tournois = 20 sous = 240 deniers. The face value of écu changed over time according to its weight and fineness. However, at the time covered by James' ledger, one écu was valued at 3 livres tournois (60 sous tournois). This information was generously supplied by Ling Li.

ANOTHER DIGRESSION: JAMES RUSHOUT IN FRANCE

What makes this sort of research fun for truly boring people is to try to answer questions that most people would never ask, let alone try to answer. This may be a section you want to skip but here's the question: Why did James take his wife to France in August 1671 and stay there long enough for their daughter Alice to be conceived and then born on June 4, 1672?[34]

Twelve letters to James from his London-based man of business, William Jarrett survive, all addressed to James c/o Monsieur Puech, an Apothecary in Montpellier.[35] The earliest are dated April 29, 1672 and November 25, 1672. For years, that was my only clue. Then I learned[36] that John Locke, the political philosopher, stayed with Puech in 1676.[37] What was Locke doing there?

Locke was an Oxford-trained physician and Montpellier is the oldest medical school in the western world. Locke left for France on November 14, 1675 and arrived back in London on May 10, 1679 and kept an extensive journal of his travels and observations. Like Pepys, Locke kept his notes in a sort of shorthand, which a Professor of French in Durham College, John Lough, largely transcribed and published.[38] Unfortunately Professor Lough did not transcribe Locke's extensive medical notes from the Journal, but there is enough transcribed to support the received wisdom that Locke treated English patients in France.[39] There is little or nothing in the partial transcription to support the other bits of received wisdom that (a) Locke augmented his medical training at Montpellier, other than by attending the odd lecture which failed to impress him, and (b) stayed in Montpellier principally to receive treatment for his own lung ailments. The suggestions are that Locke thought he might have consumption; he did seem to have had asthma

---

[34] She had to be naturalized by the House of Lords on March 12, 1677 (Gregorian) (Royal Assent 16 April 1677). That process cost James £15 which is posted in the cash ledger.

[35] Twelve letters to James survive, one dated April 29, 1672, one dated November 25, 1672, six dated October, November or December 1678 and four dated January 1679, all written from London by William Jarrett. The April 29 letter is in the London Metropolitan Archive Acc/0076. The rest are in J.P. Nelson's *Chipping Campden*. Nelson's housekeeper retrieved those letters from a bonfire at Northwick while the attics were being cleaned out after the 1964 sales. Who knows how much history was incinerated that dark day. The letters recite the granting and repayment of short term loans. For example, Mr. East (the goldsmith) paid £500 and the same day Mr. Jarrett loaned the proceeds to "Alderman Dashwood, Alderman Cervis and Mr. Robberts for 6 months at 6 p.c., no money during your absence shall be still a day". (Nelson p. 21) The letters also contain extensive reports of Parliamentary developments. It is extraordinary that as the MP for Evesham, James seems to have spent extended periods in France but clearly he was getting virtually day-by-day reports of political developments from his agent.

[36] My neighbor, friend, and aider and abettor in these endeavors, Richard Paice, gleaned this from Professor Theodore Zeldin.

[37] Dating is a problem. As we've noted, until 1752 England used the Julian calendar and, coincidentally, started the calendar year on March 25. France switched to Gregorian in the 1580s and had several years before that started the new year on January 1. The two are not linked; Julian vs. Gregorian has to do with calculating when Easter occurs, not when to start a new calendar year. So the question is: when an Englishman like Locke wrote a journal (as he did) and addressed letters, did he use the English calendar, which was by then about ten days behind, or the French? I have no idea but it matters.

[38] *Locke's Travels in France, 1675-1679*, Cambridge University Press, 1953.

[39] Indeed, Locke accompanied and attended a sickly young Englishman, Caleb Banks, and brought him to Montpellier in pursuit of a cure.

and was never very well. This might be borne out by Locke's extensive correspondence, which survives. What seems incontestable is that Montpellier (often then spelled as Montpelier) was the place to go for treatment of lung diseases in the 17th and 18th centuries.

So where does Apothicaire Puech fit in?

On Tuesday January 7, 1676 Locke reports "I removed to Mr. Puech's house… paying ten crowns per *month* for diet only. Lodging, fire & candle I had at an other place." Lough reports[40] that one "Jacques Puech, Apothicaire à Montpelier" was on the Montpellier tax rolls for 1665 as living in the Rue du puits de fer[41] with a household including "trois pensionnaires Anglois". That word "pensionnaire" does not refer to old folks on a tight budget, it indicates that Puech was running a residential hotel which was probably quite nice with rooms taken for extended periods.

The Virtues and Uses of the Queen of Hungary's Water.

THe Queen of *Hungary's* Water, being of a hot Nature, and very subtle; it strengthens the Heart, Brains and Stomach, digests all manner of Crudities, dissolves Phlegm, and repairs the Dissipations of the Spirits; in so much that one may use it for all the Indispositions of the Brains and Stomach, which may proceed from Colds, and to expel Winds and Cholicks.

To use it rightly, you must mingle half a spoonful (more or less, having respect to the Age or indisposition of the Party that is to take it) either in a little Broth, or some other Liquor, for to temper its Virtues: it may be taken several days together, or else two or three times a week.

One may also use it outwardly, for all manner of pains in what part of the Body soever; for those that are troubled with a weakness in their Sinews, to fortifie the Joynts; for the Palsie, Gout, Burnings, Contusions, and in the decline of an Erezipelus, or Saint *Anthony's* Fire. It must be used by fomenting and bathing the parts affected, warming it a little if desired. For a weakness of Sight, and the Headach, you must rub the Forehead and the Eyes. It is also very good for Deafness, in dropping it into the Ear, and stopping it with a little Wool. The Ladies use it for their Faces, it makes the skin smooth, and a fair Complexion, by taking away Scurfs or Witherness; you must wash your self twice or thrice a week by mingling it with a little Spring-water, especially those that are of a swarthy Complexion.

Amongst the several Distillers of this Water in *Montpellier*, where by the confession of all Men it is best prepared, *James Puech* Apothecary and Perfumer dwelling in the said City, doth make it with all the exactness and care imaginable; and is sold here in *London* by his Son *David Puech*, living in …

at the Sign of the true Perfumer of *Montpellier.*

Puech handbill

Locke was interested in French weights and measures and reports that on Sunday, February 16, 1676: "At Mr Pueche's we weighed a pot of their water & it weighed of Montpellier's weights 2 lbs. 14 ozs."[42]

Then we get the note "Queen of Hungary's water 40s per lb. Mr Puech"[43]. Bingo!

In 1690, a fellow named David Puech published a broadside in London called *The Virtues and Uses of The Queen of Hungary's Water.* He had a shop in London in the Haymarket where he sold the stuff produced by his father, James (Jacques), in Montpellier.

Hungary water was the first alcohol-based perfume. It seems to have principally been distilled rosemary and perhaps some thyme. It is still popular today though now as a more complex herbal. However, in the late 17th century it was the universal specific. Culpeper's *Pharmacoepia Londoniensis* (1653) says at page 60: "The Distilled water of Rosemary flowers, helps such as are troubled with the yellow Jaundice, Asthma; it cleanseth the blood, helps concoction, strengthens the brain and body exceedingly."[44]

---

[40] Ibid, p. 16, fn. 2.

[41] He also had a shop on Rue du Pas-Etroit.

[42] Ibid, p. 42.

[43] Ibid, p. 91.

[44] I have also found this, said to be in Culpeper 1693: "The water (containing an infusion of spirits) is admirable cure-all remedy of all kinds of cold and humidity-induced head ailments, apoplexies, epilepsies, dizziness, lethargy, crippleness, nerves diseases, rheumatism, flaws, spasms, loss of memory, coma, drowsiness, deafness,

Could it be that Puech was running a spa? Puech was a volume dealer in medicinals. Locke on Thursday May 21, 1676: "At Mr Puech's great quantities of Grana Kermes which they by [sic] for about 16s per lb." He goes on to explain that these are little red berries sort of like holly berries.[45]

James was unhealthy in old age; maybe it started young.[46] Was that why James was there so long with his wife and baby? Whatever the relationship was, it was not brief or casual. James' cash book contains an entry on June 15, 1677 that he paid £20:9:11 "for a bill remitted to Puech for Hungary water". The wording indicates that James paid an odd amount in sterling for a remittance to Puech in a round number of livres. Whatever the amount, it is huge. The cash book also contains an entry on June 26, 1675 indicating, if I read it correctly, that James paid £10 for a ring given to Me Puech.[47]

James also was in contact with Locke. Locke's journal contains a startling entry for Friday, March 24, 1679: "Paid Mr. Daille 100 which I received by Mr. Beaumont from Sir James Rushout."[48] In the marginal index that Locke created on each page of the journal so that he could find entries beside this little entry appears the word "Rushout". For whatever reason, Locke wanted to keep track of that little note.

There is also a line in a letter Locke wrote on December 9, 1692 explaining his care in making referrals in which he explains "I used the same measures in recommending Mr. La Treille[49] to Sir James Rushout."

Locke's letter seems to reflect an earlier incident recited in a letter from Rushout to Locke dated July 9, 1692.[50] In that letter, James thanks Locke for a favorable recommendation of Mr. La Treille, which recommendation was also endorsed by a Mr. Popple, who served with Locke on the Board of Trade and seems to have been in contact with James as well. James goes on to refer

---

ear buzzing, derangement of vision, blood coagulation, mood-induced headaches. Relieves toothache, useful for stomach cramps, pleuritis, lack of appetite, indigestion, obstruction of the liver, obstruction of the spleen, intestinal obstruction and contraction of the uterus. It receives and preserves natural heat, restores body functions and capabilities even at late age (saying has it). There are not many remedies producing that many good effects. Use internally in wine or vodka, rinse temples, breath in with your nose." I cannot find the book and the wording seems modernized, though it sounds right, and there were many later editions of Culpeper.

[45] Ibid, p. 94.

[46] James sought an ambassadorship in a warmer climate to improve his health. He seems to have tried for Italy or Portugal in 1696 and 1697 and by the time he was appointed to Constantinople he was described as "an old, rich, unhealthy gentleman" (*The House of Commons, 1690-1715, Volume I*, David Hayton *et al* p. 320). Other evidence of his ill health is that on February 27, 1670 (1671) he was given leave to be absent from the House of Commons "till he shall recover his health and be in condition to be in attendance" (*House of Commons Journal*, Volume 9), again, given leave on November 15, 1690 "to go into the country to the Bath for Six Weeks, for his health" (ibid Volume 10), again on December 19, 1692 for an unspecified period (ibid); then again on March 31, 1695 (ibid Volume 11) and for three weeks on March 10, 1696 (ibid).

[47] Today in Montpellier there is a Rue de Puech Villa which intersects with Av. des Apothicaires. In a tiny village called Le Puech about 40 miles west of Montpellier there was a famous Jardin Botanique. Puech's father, Pierre, started the family business and they seemed to have dealt in volume so maybe this is evidence that the Puechs were serious people but Puech is a very common name in the Montpellier region even today so one needs to be careful.

[48] Ibid, p. 265.

[49] I cannot identify La Treille, but there was such a person in this period who instructed in French.

[50] Bodleian: Ms. Locke c.18, f47.

to "my projects for Italy—wherein I am not determined but the apprehensions I have of another cold winter make me overcome many difficulties I foresee in the undertaking the warmer season [?] is a comfortable support to a declining constitution and the means to obtain it with most safe and speed is most desirable if it may be with any tolerable degree of prudence"—which I translate to mean that James had business in Italy which he would like to pursue and while he saw difficulties in making the trip he was willing to chance it if he could avoid another cold English winter. That confirms that James sought warmer climates for his health.

BACK TO FOLLOWING THE MONEY

A more compelling reason to think that James was not in trade is that the cash ledger contains no evidence of a purchase or sale that seems to relate to any of these foreign transactions. If James was buying silk in France and Italy, presumably he was selling it as well. Unless these foreign transactions in fact reflect a purchase and sale in the same currency we have only one side of the trade reflected in the cash ledger. That does not sound right because the Rushouts were constantly drawing amounts "in hand" for up to £200. Fifty and a hundred pounds at a clip were usual. Today that's forty and eighty thousand pounds handed over in cash. If we bear in mind that at this period and even through the 19th century, tradesman's bills were paid by the aristocracy's men of business and managers received rent, one wonders why the Rushouts received so much in cash and how they dared to carry it or even keep it in their houses. My guess is that this was largely traveling expenses.

Another transaction in the ledger of some interest is that starting on March 11, 1671, James began paying an annuity of £112.10.0 to his mother-in-law, whose name was also Alice. I don't know when James' wife's father died but in 1668, James was negotiating with Alice's mother, not her father, for her hand. The mother-in-law remarried to Mark Cottle sometime around 1671, and at that point her annuity starts to be paid to Cottle. I am simply guessing, but it sounds to me as if James bought out his mother-in-law's dower interest in the Harrow estates in exchange for the annuity. Later on, James' will reveals that he bought out his wife's dower interest in an estate so he could devise it to his son.

Some of the details in the ledgers are very interesting because they demonstrate a continuation of medieval practices. When James made a new lease, the tenant paid a "fine", which is not a punitive expression–it is simply the term for the purchase price for the privilege of entering into the lease. It would appear that some of James' estates, particularly those in Essex, were encumbered by copyhold leases which originated in the mist of time but became inheritable with the result that as the rent never changed and it depreciated, there was no point in collecting the rent and the holder of a copyhold became very close to being the owner of the land. Nevertheless, the tenant in the copyhold was subject to certain charges of which the most interesting is "heriot". Heriot entitled the landlord upon the death of the tenant to claim the tenant's best beast. This practice was an artifact held over from an earlier period when a landlord put a tenant in possession, and gave the tenant tools and some animals so upon the death of the tenant, the payment of the heriot was simply giving the landlord back something in consideration of the original supply. Over time the heriot was commuted to a liquidated sum and James collected it religiously. Another fee collected from copyholders was called "admittance." This was a fee to have another party joined as a tenant to a lease, usually the new wife of the named tenant. Originally, there was an elaborate procedure in which the named tenant would surrender the lease and have a new lease issued with his name and that of the new co-tenant so the practice was called "surrender and admittance" but it appears in James' records only as "admittance".

Whatever James did–money lending, landlording or trading, he progressed in the classic mode of merchant-trader-politician because on December 18, 1697, he was appointed Crown ambassador to Constantinople, the capital of the Levant which was breaking wide open commercially as the Ottoman empire started its decline after its defeat at the Battle of Vienna in 1683.

The Levant Company was founded originally in 1581. It competed with the East India Company (founded in 1600) trading cloth from England for a huge range of products including fruit and spices and, later in the 17th century, raw silk and finished silk goods. These trading companies had a very erratic financial history because in the wars that beset the 17th century, whatever damage was not done by the navies and privateers of a country's enemies could be done with equal frequency by pirates, especially in the Mediterranean. I do not know how James got the appointment. I see no evidence that he was a member of the Levant Company. Very few Levant Company papers survive but one volume of the Register (copies of correspondence) for the 17th century is in the National Archive (SP105/145) and no Rushout is mentioned as a governor or member of the council. On the other hand, James did have dealings with the East India Company. James' accounts for October 1667, September 1670, March 1677 and July 1677 all show financial transactions with the East India Company. One of James' surviving balance sheets dated June 24, 1674 carries as a debit "Action in the East India Company £1045". (Again note the use of the word "debit" to indicate an asset; "action" probably means shareholding.)

The fact that he was in the East India Company does not necessarily mean that he was not in the Levant Company–people were in both camps at various times–but the companies were in bitter and acrimonious competition with each other particularly during the period after 1680 when markets were shifting and both companies were trying to get into the silk trade and competitively claiming exclusive sources like Persia.

Another suggestion that James was close to the Levant Company is that his son James married the daughter of Thomas Vernon who was described as a "Turkey merchant" when he was knighted on March 8, 1685 but again, that does not necessarily mean much because merchants in this period were in each other's pockets (and beds) to an extraordinary degree. In any event the marriage occurred on February 12, 1699 (Gregorian 1700) two years after the appointment.

My guess is that James got the appointment by political pull. There is one report that James raised a regiment for William III in the Revolution. Clearly the Crown always had influence in and over the trading companies because the Crown granted the charter without which the merchants had no legal framework in which to pool their resources, other than partnerships, which ended with the death of a partner. The corporation with perpetual existence was to come in the future–the first companies had charters that expired after a term of years.

By definition the Crown could pick ambassadors because the ambassador is the personal representative of the King who is, in his person, the head of state and head of government. But the Crown was not necessarily interested in appointing ambassadors and consuls in all the places that the trading community wanted. James I said it was of no consequence to him that an ambassador should reside in Constantinople as he had no wish for friendly relations with the Turks; if the Company found an ambassador necessary for its own interests, then it must pay for him. But clearly the Crown had an interest in the commercial success of the Company both because of the duties it could exact on its trade and because the King often had a personal financial interest in the companies. For example, James I remitted the Levant Company's tax obligation on the import of currants (£5,322) for its first year of operations to help the Company meet the cost of the new present for the Ottoman Sultan. By contrast, it was thought that Charles I occasionally tipped his hand against the East India Company because he was angry that he was not allowed or given an interest in the Company. The Companies' seesaw relationship with the Crown continued through the 17th century with the merchants being continually disappointed that they could not count on the Crown to protect their trading privileges but they never stopped trying to buy protection with "loans", bargain sales of pepper, outright bribes and gifts. William and Mary are shown as having capital of £7,000 in the East India Company lists of April 18, 1691 and April 18, 1693. I venture to guess that these capital accounts were gifts, not paid-in capital, though they shared in the profits with the other proprietors.

Starting in 1691, William III began to appoint ambassadors to Constantinople without consulting the Levant Company. Men of rank competed for the position because while an ambassador could not trade in competition with the Company, he could traffic in jewels and foreign exchange and he could import large quantities of wine duty-free, which he could sell (not all Turks followed the dictates of the Muslim religion in this regard). He could also do a lucrative trade in "baraks", which seem to have been a form of diplomatic immunity intended to be conferred on the ambassador's personal retinue but could also be sold to men of wealth resident in the empire whose positions were insecure, such as Armenians, Greeks and Jews. This is a record of one barak trading at £2,000. Depending on the ebb and flow of his power, the King had more or less influence on the award of the ambassadorship. I think that William appointed James Rushout as ambassador without consulting the Company because in 1699, after James died without taking up his appointment, the Levant Company formally petitioned the King to be allowed to choose the successor (nothing happened; Rushout's predecessor stayed in place).

James was an active politician serving on many parliamentary committees over almost three decades in the House. He was considered a reliable supporter of the Crown, which favors my guess that the ambassadorial appointment was a political, rather than commercial, preferment. William III's letter to the Company advising them of James Rushout's appointment and telling them to get on with the usual details reeks of prerogative.[51] On the occasion of his appointment as ambassador, James entered into a contract with the Levant Company to represent the interests of the Company.[52] The contract called for him to be paid £600 toward the expense of fitting out for the trip; £500 for "entertainment money at his first coming thither"; 8,000 "royalls of eight" in each of the succeeding five years, and £300 to get back to England as well as a huge allowance of duty free wine, secretarial services, salaries of three "Drugermen"[53] etc. Poor James did not live

---

[51] By April 15, 1697 the Levant Company had written a long letter to the King complaining that the East India Company was interfering with their exports of English woolens to Persia and by July 15, 1697 the Governor and Council were working on a long letter to the King suggesting instructions to be given to the new ambassador by the King. These instructions largely consisted of remonstrating with the Sultan over unauthorized duties being imposed on the Company's trade (bribes? extortion?). But the draft letter comes to an end noting that Rushout had died. This same volume in the Archive contains many other letters to the King suggesting instructions to be given to ambassadors all dealing with the nitty-gritty of trade in a literally cut-throat arena. The index to the records for this period seems fragmentary but none of the secondary sources, including an exhaustive Ph.D thesis on the Levant Company in this period lodged in the Guildhall Library, mentions Rushout. As noted, James' surviving personal balance sheets and accounts show no investment in the Levant Company.

[52] The contract is dated January 5, 1697 whereas his appointment as ambassador is dated December 18, 1697, at first perplexing except because of Julian dating, the contract is January 5, 1698 and so properly after his appointment in December 1697.

[53] A drugerman (dragoman) is an interpreter (cultural guide plus language interpreter). Today dragomen will show you around the Pyramids or the temples at Luxor but in the 17th century they were absolutely essential intermediaries and advisors to people such as Rushout who, with no experience of the Levant, was going to show

long enough to cash in; he died in 1698 before departing England. At least his wife, Alice, got a bit out of it; she received a gold beaker with the arms of the Levant company on it–apparently a customary gift to ambassadors' wives.

Rushout beaker

This became known as the Rushout Beaker; it sold on November 20, 2001 at Christie's King Street London for £300,750 including buyer's premium.

---

up with his wife in what we now call Turkey knowing nothing of the local languages, customs, politics, trade, etc., It was a very dangerous place. At a minimum dragomen "conveyed messages and served as a channel of communication". In reality they were intelligence agents. Italian was the *lingua franca* of the Levant and most of the dragomen were of Italian extraction. Since they were the subjects of the Sultan and by definition knew how to get along, they played a very interesting, if not to say, Byzantine role.

THE HARROW CONNECTION

I mentioned above that James' wife, Alice Pitt, was heir to the estate at Harrow-on-the-Hill. This fact warrants a bit of a digression at this point because James became the Lord of the Manor of Harrow, a subject of some, well at least a little, interest. A lordship of a manor was an extraordinarily complex feudal construct. It seems to have been an inheritable status given by the King that passed with title to designated lands and it seems to have involved, among other things, the right and duty to run a manorial judicial court. Harrow was a manor, and as Alice's husband, James succeeded to the Lordship upon the death of Alice's father. Northwick was not a manor. The incidents of manorial lordship were clearly very complicated.

An illustration of how complicated came up with respect to the duty to repair the chancel at Harrow church. Vicars of churches held land, which came with their position, which produced an income to fund the vicar's responsibility for the upkeep of the chancel (mainly roof repair) while the rest of the church was the responsibility of the parish. Henry VIII confiscated the properties of most large religious houses (such as monasteries, abbeys, convents and priories) and sold them, and when the confiscated property included a church used by the parish, the responsibility for chancel upkeep passed to the purchasers of the vicars' parcels. The purchasers became known as lay rectors.

The Bishop of Oxford and the Dean and Chapter of the Cathedral Church of Christ in Oxford, owned and leased to Sir Francis Gerard the "Great Tithes" within the parish of Harrow, meaning that Gerard owned the Church's claim to a portion of the value of hay, corn and wood grown within the parish.[54] James, on the other hand, must have succeeded to confiscated titles of the rectory, glebe land (land the products of which support parish charities), chancel and parsonage, presumably because James' predecessor in interest was a customer or friend of Henry VIII. The question was who had the duty to repair the chancel. Why this was a question if indeed James was a lay rector escapes me, but in 1661 the Dean and Chapter of Christchurch, Oxford

---

[54] The subject of tithes deserves its own boring footnote. From before the Norman Conquest it was customary to pay 10% of the "profits" of lands and "the industry of parishioners" for the maintenance of the parish priest. This was not an *ad valorem* tax; it was an income tax. So-called "predial" tithes were imposed on the products of the soil. "Mixed tithes" were the produce of animals including their young, and by-products such as milk, wool and eggs. Personal tithes arose wholly from labor and were also based on clear profit, not gross income. Tithes on corn, grain, hay and wood were called "Great Tithes"; everything else was a small tithe. The difference was important. Originally most tithes were payable to the rector of the parish but these tithes over time were appropriated and annexed to bishops or institutions such as monasteries who in turn appointed a person called a "vicar" to do the actual parish work in return for the "small tithes".

When Henry VIII dissolved the religious houses after 1535, he acquired their tithe rights as well, and sometimes sold them off or gave them away as a form of inheritable personal property passing under the rules of primogeniture. Other tithes remained Crown property. Thus, the right to the tithes often passed to a person who might not be the rector or vicar of the parish. When the owner was not the cleric, the owner had to establish a stipend for a perpetual cleric. Inevitably tensions arose because the people getting the money tried to keep as much of it as possible and clergy were impoverished and church property became dilapidated. In 1704 Queen Anne agreed to cede the Crown's share of the tithes to a fund called "Queen Anne's Bounty" to assist the poorer clergy and the whole business became quite bureaucratic. Though Queen Anne undoubtedly had higher motives, supporting the clergy was also necessary because the clergy were both spiritual and community leaders and as they were among the few educated people in the countryside, much local administration including poor relief and road repair was in their hands. Even today, the local governmental unit in England is called a Parish with a Parish Council which has nothing to do with the church. Starting in the 18th century and particularly in the 19th and early 20th century, these tithes were commuted to fixed fees paid in cash and were administered by the government as a tax. The obligation to pay tithes could also be bought out for a lump sum. If this subject fascinates you and you have no life at all, the best source for further reading is *The Law Relating to Tithe Rent Charge*, Percy William Millard, Butterworth, London, 2nd Edition 1926.

demanded that Edward Palmer (Alice's first husband) and Alice get on with the chancel repairs. There ensued a bizarre litigation, involving Gerard for some reason, which got pretty hot in 1664. It seems to have been settled in 1666 with each side (Gerard and Pitt) paying half but the issue came up again and on December 12, 1676, the Bishop of Oxford wrote to James Rushout, Palmer's successor, saying that the chancel was in such need of repair that soon the question "will be, not who is to repair but who is to build the chancel". The Bishop noted that the other party, Sir Francis Gerard, was willing to have the matter arbitrated. On January 2, 1676, James replied to the Bishop saying that the Bishop had been sold a bill of goods and the chancel was not in such bad shape. It is a very snippy letter, with James suggesting that there are troublemakers afoot stirring up controversy and besmirching his reputation. It was all finally settled in a tripartite agreement dated January 10, 1677 following an arbitration which split the baby 50/50. The parties settled with the Dean extending Gerard's lease of the Great Tithes forever on condition that the lessee pays half the cost of maintaining the chancel. Sir James agreed to pay the other half.[55]

Just as there could be squabbles about a tithe owner's duty to repair a part of a church, so too there were squabbles about other duties. In 1686 James Rushout was indicted by the attorney general for failing to repair certain bridges at Pinner, which was part of the Harrow estate. File 76/1649-56 in the London Metropolitan Archive contains a note of the indictment and a list of bridges and what seems to be James' handwritten comments about each of them. There ensued a jury trial with testimony about the tradition of who repaired what in which it was mentioned that Alice's father, Edward Pitt, had repaired one of them which indicates that tradition counted. The case seems to have gone against James.

Turning now to James' involvement with Northwick, James took title to Northwick in 1682 (Gregorian) and later expanded the estate, buying several large farms.

James had been an MP for Evesham since 1670 and might have had a passing familiarity with his constituency though that was not a requirement of the position and, as noted above, he was in France for extended periods. He had inherited from his father, John I, some former Courteen estates near Evesham. There is speculation that his family roots in textiles meant that he saw the Cotswolds as being of commercial interest. There is also speculation that since silk throwing began in Blockley after James arrived, *post hoc propter hoc*. Silk throwing was a very low-tech process of taking the hanks of silk filament which had been unwound from the cocoons in the country of origin and shipped to England in large bales, washing them and spinning them into threads of various dimensions (warp and weft were differently sized). It was a cottage industry and a silk mill originally was simply a warehouse and office where the cottagers brought their output of thread and picked up more hanks. Silk throwing was done all over England using conventional spinning wheels. Eventually machines were developed but that came later (though Leonardo da Vinci had designed one). James Rushout did buy a mill in Blockley which became the first silk throwing mill but that seems to have started in 1700 after James' death and in any event the Rushouts acquired most of Blockley so the acquisition of a mill, *per se*, means nothing. Further, even if the mill was a "spinning mill" in 1688, that does not necessarily mean silk—wool would be more likely. A mill is a mill and over time they changed output from grain to textiles.

---

[55] It was not until October 13, 2013 that Parliament finally minimized the chances that one could unwittingly become a lay rector with liability for chancel repairs. From that date, the parochial claim for chancel upkeep has to be registered in the land records before the burdened parcel is next sold. If the claim is registered or the parcel is given away, not sold, the claim persists. There are parcels which will remain subject to the burden forever.

James' residence in Montpellier on the trade route to Lyon, the silk center, is also highly suggestive and his account book may admit some textile dealing. But this much is clear: it is the weavers who count in silk making, not the throwers. The great weavers were largely Huguenot refugees who settled in Spitalfields and got their thread from many sources. Blockley's thread mainly was sent to ribbon makers in Coventry. The notion that James introduced a marvelous, highly skilled trade to the town because of his experience in textiles is probably fiction; there is no evidence that silk weaving was ever done in Blockley.

Furthermore, unlike his father, James was not a commercial mover and shaker. He was neither a governor nor a member of the board of the East India Company and his surviving papers betray no substantial commercial activity–they reveal mainly real property matters and money lending. Also, very importantly, James' father, John, had been barred by his letters of denization from acting as a merchant (which is what starting a silk throwing mill would be) and had made his way in the merchant adventurer class. It would be surprising for James to move backward into trade. Rather he promoted himself as a gentleman, a Baronet, and by the end of his life was, a Lieutenant-Colonel in a Regiment of Foot in the Worcestershire Militia.

THE ORIGINS OF NORTHWICK PARK

When old farts write of what happened in one place over millennia, it is apparently obligatory to start, if not with primordial slime, then at least with early men or man-like bipeds. O.K. There are Neolithic sites for religious ceremonies all over Gloucestershire and some unproven indications of Neolithic occupation at Aston Magna, about two miles from Northwick. But I can't relate to those folk so let's move on.

For reasons no one has adequately explained, Julius Caesar tried to invade Britain in 55 B.C. and failed. Ninety years later, Claudius tried again and had better luck (maybe the elephants he brought to scare the natives did the trick). The Romans, perhaps searching in vain for a decent plate of pasta or a drinkable wine, then pushed north and along the way they built roads, one of which, built about 47 A.D., is now called the Fosse Way. It began in Cirencester (f/k/a Corinium) and ran along what is now the A429 road out of Moreton-in-Marsh. Along that route, two miles southeast of Northwick, the Romans built the village of Dorn, perhaps as a market town. The settlement consisted of 10 acres enclosed by a massive bank and ditch system, which served as defenses. Clearly the town was still thriving in the 4th century as lots of coins and pottery from that period have been found. We don't know what happened to Dorn when the Saxon invaders came, their approach from the sea possibly aided by that fine road. If Dorn was populated by retired German troops (the Romans hired local talent everywhere), maybe they got on well enough.

The Saxons settled. There's a Saxon burial ground in downtown Blockley. The area was absorbed into the kingdom of Mercia in the 7th century. A Christian community developed by the 9th century under the aegis of what became the bishopric of Worcester. In the year 855, the king of the Mercians needed to raise funds to fight off the invading Danes so he sold a missionary outpost in a place called Bloccanleeh and the land that endowed it to Bishop Ealhun of Worcester for 300 silver shillings. The Bishop of Worcester thus acquired the customary rights that over the years evolved into the lordship of the manor. By 964, the Bishop tacked on to his Blockley manor another nearby estate he owned called Northwick—the name simply meaning the "north farm or settlement" as it was even then a cluster close to, but north of, Blockley. Until 1931, the parish and manor of Blockley were in Worcestershire, not Gloucestershire, simply because the majority of the land was owned by the Bishop of Worcester. This is the reason there is no picture of Northwick in Kip's great work *The Ancient and Present State of Gloucestershire*, which pictures many of the great estates in Gloucestershire. Northwick was clearly otherwise eligible for the treatment though not grand enough for Kip's *Britannia Illustrata*. In 1906, the Bishops of Worcester ceased to be the patrons of the living of Blockley in a shuffle of ecclesiastical rights, which was followed in 1919 by a transfer of the ecclesiastical parish to the diocese of Gloucester. The civil parish became part of Gloucestershire in 1931. The lordship of the manor of Blockley was functionally dissolved by the 1850s though the empty shell is still held by the Ecclesiastical Commissioners.

The ecclesiastical parish of Blockley is an enclave and if we start a circle on Broad Campden Hill, it ran a bit east of what is now the A44 road, down about a mile and then east above Batsford, then down to Dorn (a narrow finger pierced from there down beyond Moreton-in-Marsh), then over to Ditchford, north to Ebrington, down to include Paxford and over the top of Northwick Park back to Broad Campden Hill.

The manor of Blochelei was valued in the Domesday Book, drawn up in 1086, at about twice the size and value of Chipping Campden. It was said to contain 63 "hides", 38 in Blockley and 25 in Northwick. Authorities opine on the size of a "hide" but I know of no really reliable guess. The consensus suggests about a hundred arable acres with a wide variation seeming to relate to the ease with which the land could be plowed.

By 1182, Northwick itself was held as a knight's fee (meaning an inheritable leasehold which was deemed to produce sufficient income to support a knight) by Roger de Norwycke and others of that surname. It was split among his heirs and not reunited until 1383 when a local man, John Childe, acquired it and thus began three centuries of almost uninterrupted Childe family control. William Childe succeeded to the estate in 1583 and it is suggested that he then built what are now the older parts of the Northwick Mansion, which seems to be a reasonable inference if we assume that the Mansion's stepped gables were part of that development. The reports of William are pretty thin but we know that he claimed arms, served as a county magistrate and was twice high sheriff of Worcestershire.

By this time, Northwick Park was a recognized landmark. It is pinpointed and named as "Northwick" on Saxton's map of Gloucestershire of 1577 and Speed's maps of Worcestershire and Gloucestershire done in 1610 (in all cases, of course, as an enclosure of Worcestershire within Gloucestershire).[56] It also features on the Sheldon Tapestry of Worcestershire, which was created in the late 16th century.

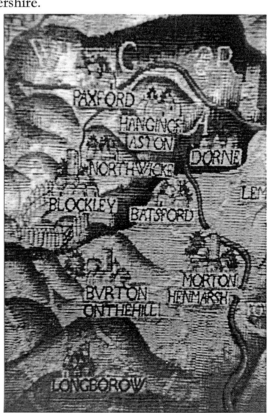

The Sheldon Tapestry

One interesting 16th-century sidelight on Northwick and its surroundings occurs in the journals of John Dee, a then-famous Elizabethan mathematician, navigator, astrologer, seer and alchemist. In March 1583, Dee notes that his assistant and a certain Mr. John Hysey of Blockley had by "spiritual guides" (*i.e.,* spirits) been directed to find "a certain muniment of a book and a scroll found in Northwick Hill." The scroll was written in a "strange" language; the "muniment" was a manuscript, part of *The Book of Dunstan*, attributed to St. Dunstan, a 10th-century bishop of Worcester, London and Canterbury, and some-time Abbot of Glastonbury who was reputed to be an alchemist. Dee

---

[56] Why was it so singled out? Perhaps, as with the Kips, so the owner would buy the atlas? As I can testify, if you are a truly boring person, finding your house featured in the oldest printed maps of England has a distinct loosening effect on the purse strings.

proclaimed that powder found with the book was an alchemical elixir and was convinced the scroll was a treasure map. The ensuing diary entries dealing with Dee's consultations with spirits are a fascinating insight into the Elizabethan mind, quite tortured by a combination of religious, mystical and magical beliefs, which the Elizabethans firmly held and acted upon. Indeed, you will never understand Elizabethan politics and society until you understand that they really believed this stuff–a mass delusion if you will.

The next event of note was the bubonic plague in 1637, when the normal death rate of thirty per year leapt to fifty-seven.

Another of the four horsemen arrived with the Civil War. Blockley (and Worcestershire) were largely on the royalist side. Late in the war the King's troops were quartered beside St James Church in Chipping Campden and behaved rather oppressively. It all came to an end with the last battle of the first phase of the Civil War on March 21, 1646 when the troops quartered in Campden marched to reinforce the King at Oxford and were finally stopped at Stow-in-the-Wold after a running battle through Donnington and Longborough.

THE BISHOP'S LEASES AND TITLE TO THE ESTATE AND MANSION

The Bishops of Worcester milked Blockley for income (they owned large flocks of sheep raised for wool)[57] and used it as a way station on their travels to London. They had a manor house in what is now the center of town but for whatever reason, they lost interest in the place and by 1500 began to put out parts of the manor on long leases.

My only information on the early leases is: "Towards the end of the tenth century we find Oswald, Bishop of Worcester, explaining in a letter to King Edgar his practice of letting church lands to a tenant for three lives (the lives being the tenant's own, and those of two other persons named by him as successors) on terms of rendering specified services…"[58] Early leases may be found in the Worcester Records Office but I can't read them because they are written in early forms of court hand and obscurely formulaic Latin, so I am unaware of the contents of any of the leases before September 10, 1588, when the Bishop granted Queen Elizabeth a lease for 99 years to commence upon the expiration in February 1639 of a lease to the then current tenant. I think there must have been some uncertainty about the validity of this lease because by a lease dated 13 October 1589, the Bishop leased to the Queen a "messuage [a dwelling house and outbuildings] and 3 yard lands" occupied by Francis Hunks. There followed a strange, multi-step transaction which might have been a medieval way of quieting title to the leasehold. First, on October 31, 1589, the Queen assigned her leasehold interests to Roger Lopez, her physician, probably as a gift for services rendered. Then nine days later on November 9, 1589, Lopez assigned his leasehold interest to John Throckmorton and Edward King who in turn surrendered the leasehold to the Bishop three days later on November 12, 1589. The next day, November 13, 1589, the Bishop granted a new lease to the Queen, this time for ninety years to begin when the current lease (presumably to Hunks) expired in 1639. On December 17, 1591 the Queen again assigned the leasehold to Throckmorton and another man (whose name I cannot read but may be King) in trust for Lopez. Throckmorton and King may have been nominal parties with no real interest who simply acted as a conduit to overcome some legal problem.

Lopez was a Portuguese Jew who was very well regarded. He was appointed Elizabeth's physician in 1586, two years before the Armada but by February 1594 in some sort of court intrigue, Lopez was accused, probably falsely, of having tried to poison the Queen and being a Spanish collaborator. He was conveniently tried and convicted so that he could be executed at Tyburn on November 19, 1594 without a warrant from the Queen who tended to dither over signing death warrants. Others took over his leasehold but on November 19, in the eighth year (1633) of "Charles the First (of blessed memory) the said Roger Lopez was found to be aliene borne[59] by reason whereof his then present Majesty Charles the First was rightfully entitled to said lease" and "all assignments and grants since made of said lease were absolutely void against

---

[57] Cotswold sheep produced a wool that lent itself to making broadcloth, a heavy fabric created by beating the cloth so that the warp and weft are indistinguishable. Unfortunately, the wool was not good for the succeeding fashion, the thinner worsted, so the trade crashed in the 17th century and was decimated by 1680. An interesting question is why the Cotswold sheep farmers didn't adapt.

[58] Frederick Pollock, *The Land Laws*, Macmillan, 1883 (reprinted by Elibron Classics), pp. 260-261.

[59] Aliens could not own real estate; that is one of the reasons they sought denization.

his present Majesty". The next assignment of the leasehold we see is by Charles I on 29 November 1635 (tenth year) when it went back into private hands.

I do not know what land the lease(s) encompassed but the assignment to Lopez describes lots including "Blockley Park," land in the "hamlet of Aston", thirteen yards in Paxford, a watermill in Draycott and land in Teddington–all subject to the continuing customary tenancies. I think that the Bishop owned outright the bulk of the land in the Blockley enclave of Worcestershire in Gloucestershire as shown on the Saxton map of 1586 and he leased it all.

Well, not quite all because the Bishop did not own the Northwick Mansion. That "knight's fee" of Roger de Norwyke must have converted to something along the lines of what we now call a fee simple. After the Norman Conquest, William I regarded all of England as his by conquest and he made conditional grants of bits and pieces to others who would do him service such as providing five knights to fight for him forty days a year. There evolved from this simple scheme an incredibly elaborate lacework of tenancies under which everyone held a bit of land on condition that they do something for their immediate overlord. This became a mess of conditional tenures requiring all sorts of exotic services and reserving all manner of rights if certain eventualities occurred. It became very difficult to convey land–no one could know with certainty who was to do what for whom. Further, some of the conditions of service were commuted to fixed payments, which, over time, with inflation, became worthless. Attempts were made to simplify this in a Puritan Parliament in 1647 (confirmed in 1660 on the Restoration) and a few times in the 19th century, but it was not until 1925 that Parliament said 'Enough!' and simplified things so that most land is now held in what is called freehold or more accurately "fee simple".

Leaseholds evolved as contractual rights to occupy land that someone else owned. Leases of 100 years at fixed rents were common and the combination of uncertainty about who the landlord was and the effects of inflation making the rent not worth collecting meant that properties tended to evolve from leaseholds to freeholds either by purchase or abandonment or, possibly, adverse possession.

Medieval land tenure is murky at best and the great experts of the 18th and 19th century disagreed with each other about its incidents so I have no hope of understanding the Northwick leaseholds in detail but I am certain that the Mansion was not leased. The May 8, 1683 deed by William Childe, son and heir of Thomas Childe in consideration of £14,000 paid to Thomas Stephens and Richard Jenkinson[60] pursuant to an indenture dated February 14, 1680 (1681) "bargained and sold" to James Rushout the "Manor or Lordship of Northwick" and "the site of the said Manor or Capital Messaunge or chief Mansion house of Northwick" and appurtenant land known as "Blockley Meadow" which ran to the "Oxford Highway" (which I think is the road over the hill to Broad Campden, not the A44), which specifically says "being freehold and not leasehold", suggests it contained 450 acres. Why else would James Rushout pay such a fortune?[61]

---

[60] Thomas Childe was married to Anne Marie Jenkinson who died on February 11, 1659 (1660) and while Thomas did not die until 1679, maybe the Jenkinson family had some sort of dower interest which accounts for part of the purchase price going to a Jenkinson. By the way, the redoubtable John Haggart figured out that Anne Marie's memorial is on the north wall of St Peter and St. Paul's church in Blockley–the lady lying on a couch.

[61] Northwick was not a manor. Though the term has been indiscriminately applied to large estates, technically a manor was a juridical unit with the lord having power to adjudicate some small criminal and civil matters and,

What actually happened was that Thomas Childe, who acquired the property from his father in 1635, began to mortgage it heavily in 1664 (the mortgages in this period read as grants for 99, 500 or even 1000 years but they were redeemable) and under his will the property was conveyed to trustees by a decree in chancery, for the trustees to sell it to pay the debts. It seems that James Rushout contracted through his man of business, William Jarret, to buy the property but did so by paying off the mortgagees directly, one by one, over a couple of years.

Conveyancing in England until recently was not accomplished merely by delivery of a deed; it required a ceremonial act–even the handing over of a handful of dirt or the hinge of a building but much more importantly, required entering into possession or "seizin". There is a lovely illustration of this in a letter that James Rushout wrote to his agent Jarret, in February 1681 telling him how to take possession: "I here enclosed send you a note from Mr Stephens and Mr. Freeman [Thomas Childe's trustees] whereby Gilson the bailiff is directed to deliver possession of the establishment to my Agent I desire you would take some understanding man with you and take possession of it in my name in this manner (*viz.*). Let the bailiff and all his family go out of the great house and deliver you the keys thereof declaring that by direction of the Trustees he doth deliver you possession of that house and of the whole Manor of Northwick for my use, this being done you may call him in again and declare that you place him there as my servant to keep possession for me and to deliver out Nothing belonging to the house without my pr ily [unclear in original] and direction. Then I desire you to take an Inventory of the Lumber and wainscot and such other things as you think might reasonably be expected to be left there and leaving a copy with him send me a Duplicate of it."[62]

James Rushout also acquired leaseholds. In his accounts for 1689, James Rushout records that he is paying the Bishop £22.15.6 and paying a tithe to the vicar of £18.7.8. which seems to have been rent on some leaseholds. When James' son John Rushout III entered into a marriage settlement with the Earl of Northampton to marry Anne Compton, it is recited that some part of Northwick is on lease from the Bishop of Worcester. This much is clear: John III acquired the Lopez leasehold by assignment dated January 27, 1730 (1731) paying £300 for it which seems like a lot of money for an expiring leasehold but maybe it gave him a right to renew. At any rate the Lopez leaseholds became part of the Rushout-held leaseholds at that time.[63]

This mention of £14,000 as the cash portion of the purchase price raises the question: How much would that be today? The National Archive suggests a multiple of 83.54 for a 1680 pound which would be £1,169,560 in 2005. An impression of comparative value can be gleaned from the accounts of the churchwardens of St. James, a large church in Chipping Campden. The church wardens were responsible for the maintenance of the fabric of the church and its decoration as well as the churchyard and its walls and gates. Their accounts over the years include

---

rather importantly, keeping records of who owned or leased what real property. Most medieval and later leases would be noted on the manorial roll (literally as much as forty-three feet of parchments stitched together and rolled up) and the tenant proved his rights by retaining a scrap of parchment which was a copy of the entry on the manorial roll with the result that his tenancy came to be called a "copyhold". Blockley was a manor and the Bishop held manorial courts there into the mid-19th century.

[62] I am indebted to John Haggart for this transcription of the original.

[63] By lease dated May 9, 1770 the Bishop leased to John Rushout for three lives a "stable and coach house lately built North of Blockley Church" and all fishing and hunting in the Manor of Blockley plus fifty acres known as Moreland ground, twenty acres "by Paxford Brook" and the Stapenhill Farm for an annual rent of £6.34. Presumably a premium was paid for the lease.

occasional small gifts to the poor and replacement of altar cloths as well as fees for killing nuisance birds, "urchins" (hedgehogs), badgers and other varmints. Communion wine was a large part of the budget. The detail of the accounts is largely unfathomable to me but as magnitudes, they are indicative of costs and inflation. I selected the following annual totals as the dates approximate the dates of other expenditures mentioned in this book and as you see a sum mentioned, it might help if you look back to this table.[64]

1626	£ 14
1648	£ 28
1681	£ 25
1724	£ 34
1800	£ 45
1821	£117
1859	£237

---

[64] *The General Accounts of the Churchwardens of Chipping Campden 1626 to 1907*, Campden Record Series, 1992.

THE HISTORY OF THE MANSION

The Mansion and greenhouse, as viewed from the southwest.

When I first moved to Northwick, I was perplexed that the splendid architecture was on the rear of the house and the front was, well, badly butchered. I speculated that in the early 18th century the approach to the house had been diverted to the west, and I looked for evidence for this, thus avoiding the obvious: if you were a wealthy lender buying an unprepossessing one-hundred-year-old house in the middle of nowhere and wanting to make your entry into the landed gentry with a bit of a splash, what would you do? The house is small. It makes sense that the first thing you would do is to build a greenhouse to be able to support your lifestyle in an age without farmers' markets and, if you needed to increase the cube of the rather modest structure, you would install an up-to-date façade while you were at it. That the owner starts the new look on the rear is the best argument for his having done structural in-filling work behind the new façade. He must have intended to do something even more pretentious on the front but never got around to it.

It has been suggested that William Childe largely reconstructed the Mansion in the 1580s as the rectangular block we see today with its stepped gables but that it was U-shaped on the west (looking up the hill) and that someone filled in the U to create a solid block.[65] I have never had the opportunity to crawl inch-by-inch over the Mansion to try to figure out what the construction sequence was and it may well be that the recent conversion has made that a pointless exercise. There is a physical fact that supports the 'fill-in' theory: the pedimented western façade is late-

[65] R. Wittoker, 'Lord Burlington at Northwick Park' in H. Colvin & J. Harris (eds.), *The Country Seat,* 1970, pp. 121-30. Nicholas Kingsley in *The Country Houses of Gloucestershire, Vol. II* suggests it was L-shaped with ranges on east and south, p. 188.

17th-century, as is the greenhouse. "Orangerie" is the label put on the structure by a late-20th-century sales promoter–the family inventories starting in 1705 call it the "greenhouse".

In 1988 and 1989 while the Mansion was being re-constructed, staff members of the Royal Commission on the Historical Monuments of England wrote an "Historic Building Report" on the Mansion ("Report"). Because large amounts of the plaster within the house had fallen away or been removed, they were able to see where doors and windows had been removed over the years and they reached two principle conclusions: First, the house was L-shaped (the south and east ranges) before the western façade was added and second, the towers on the east façade were added before Burlington worked on the house. Indeed their view was that Burlington's work was largely decorative–plasterwork, moving interior partitions around, *etc.*

I cannot add anything to the debate other than some words of caution. It is reasonable to believe that there has been a house on the Mansion site for the better part of a thousand years. Craftsmen, particularly masons, re-use as much material as possible so crawling around in an old cellar will certainly tell you that something has changed but when and why it changed is the hard question.

Visible evidence for the "L" camp is that there is a vertical break in the northern façade that could have been a corner and the gables on the north façade are different from those on the east and west. Against that, however, is that the Dutch gables on the east and west all seem to date from the same period and to have worn equally. There is also the anomaly that in hearth assessments in 1671 and 1674 fourteen chimneys were recorded and the Report can only account for twelve in the putative L-shaped section so they assume two in outbuildings. But if the house was U-shaped, fourteen might be right.

Cellar stairs in kitchen annex

In plans from the mid-18th century, an exit from the north side of the house is shown with an indication of a bit of a wall proceeding from the north façade. One plan indicates this is a corridor to the kitchen. My guess is that there was something there because James II's inventory of 1705 (discussed below) segues from rooms that were clearly in the main house to rooms that were essential to the house operation and not clearly stated to be outbuildings. Pretty clearly inventoried are the contents "In Mrs. Down's Room over the Plowman's Hall" which were the items entrusted to a senior servant such as a housekeeper or lady's maid. Mrs. Downs had a fireplace, feather bed and a trunk marked AR with contents suggesting the cast-off clothes of a wealthy woman. She also kept the family linen in her possession. The kitchen and scullery and "Meale Chamber" seem to have been in the same structure as were several wine, beer and ale "sellers". There are cellars of some antiquity under parts of Burlington Court that would still serve admirably as wine cellars. I have no idea how old those cellars are but would confidently guess at a date before 1600, perhaps much earlier. The stairs to that cellar show years of wear, surely hundreds of years.

The technique of building the cellar is also very old. The box-like patches on the columns in the pictures below are where indentations called "putlog-holes" have recently been filled. Rather than build from the floor a supporting frame on which to lay the arch stones, supports were stretched between points just below the intended shoulder of the arch to create a platform on which the arch stones were laid. The supports slid into those holes (hence the name, which is genuine).

Kitchen cellar

Putlog-holes

That this construction technique was used does not advance our speculations about the age of the cellar except to establish that there is no relevant "not before" date. The technique goes back to the earliest medieval development of the arch and could have been used last Tuesday, because it works.[66]

So maybe the earliest significant dwelling was on the northwest corner of Burlington Court over that very old cellar. Maybe Childe started anew to the south with the much larger house and connected it to the old house, which was turned into a service wing. That might explain the thickness of the foundation.

The original structure would not have been two stories above ground; as a second story was added, they would have enlarged the foundation and reclad the whole structure[67]–again suggesting a service wing that was enlarged. It is also clear that the roof of the wing has changed–the

---

[66] See: *The Construction of Gothic Cathedrals*, John Fitchen, University of Chicago Press, 1981, particularly Appendix B.

[67] Curiously, the quality of the external stone work on the wing changes. The north façade in particular goes from a crude, almost rubble work on the west to ashlar on the east. The rubble is at the second story level over that old cellar. This mystified me for years until my neighbor Betina Goodall reported that she met the last developer of Northwick Park at a party and he reported that section of wall fell down as they were rebuilding the unit and they patched it together as quickly as possible.

marks of a lower roof being affixed to the Mansion are evident. Alternatively, the thick foundation is a red herring: Early masons had no way of calculating loads and learned not to skimp on foundations, especially in the clay which underlies Northwick.

The 1705 inventory does not mention any contents in the "Plowman's Hall". I speculate that it was probably an estate management office where the tenants came to pay their rent and otherwise do business with the landlord. These sorts of facilities were a regular feature of later country houses and the practice had to start sometime.

We know James I bought the house in 1683. Clearly James intended that Northwick would be his real home. On 14 October 1690 he contracted with the Blockley village church for a family vault on the east side of the chancel. He had to indemnify the church against damage to the foundation from the creation of the vault. The Worcestershire Record Office contains a lot of routine correspondence to James addressed to Northwick; clearly he lived there more than occasionally. James' will dated October 23, 1691 (in which he identifies himself as being "of Northwick in the County of Worcestershire") authorizes his executors to lay out "any sums not exceeding two hundred pounds if they shall think be fitting towards the finishing of my said dwelling house and for the building and finishing of walls and other necessary openings in and about my garden house and my [unclear word] courts and gardens". He left his wife the use of the house and its contents, outbuildings, gardens and orchards "until some son of my body begotten shall attain the age of one and twenty years or my said wife shall remarry…"

His will thus confirms James I as the re-builder/builder of Northwick and ratifies the declaration on the rain collector of the west façade "1686 IR" (the "I" being pretentious Latin for Iacobus or James). The will also shows him to be quite vain. He instructs his executors to manage his funeral "without the vain and useless pomp of a publick solemnity" "nor more expense made than such as may consist of the [unclear] of a private internment." He leaves £20 per annum to be distributed "among such poor inhabitants of the said parish of Blockley as are proper objects of charity and have never received that weekly [?] alms of said parish and no other persons whatsoever…" This annual dole ends when the first of his surviving sons reaches the age of 24. He also gives £20 to be distributed "among such poor people as come to my funeral at Blockley." His "deare wife" gets £200 "to buy mourning for herself and my unmarried children and as many of my servants as she shall think fitting." Others are given significant bequests to buy mourning. All this from a man who would avoid "vain and useless pomp" and have a private internment.

The will also reveals James as a control freak. His father John I's will is largely devoted to myriad bequests, large and small, which indicate a sense of duty to his church and wish to have friends and servants know that he thought fondly of them. There is little of that with James. Instead James goes on for ten or more pages making it clear that his enumerated properties must go to his first born son and that son's lawfully begotten sons in order, failing which the will rattles on with other enumerated successors and their sons each to the "third, fourth, fifth, sixth and seventh and all and every other son and sons." That's classic "entailing"; control by will or deed of the order of succession to title to real property.

James' will recites deals made with his wife to buy out her dower interest for an annuity of £600 per annum. His two younger sons, John and George, get £100 each for life but if they try to mortgage or convey that annuity, it is void (a spendthrift trust in 1691!).

At any rate, when James died in 1697 and Alice died a month or two later, the house was still unfinished.

In 1677, James I and Alice had a son, the 2nd Baronet also called James (James II).[68]

James II married Arabella, daughter of Thomas Vernon in February 1699 (1700). James I had executed an extraordinary codicil to his will on February 14, 1697 in which he recites "since the making of my said will I have some reason to doubt that my son James either is married or may hereafter marry in my lifetime without my consent or may marry after my death with some person unsuitable to his circumstances in the world to the damage and disparagement of himself and family" and went on to provide that all of the bequests to his son would be suspended "until his marriage to some person whose present fortune either in land or money is worth at least £5000" and he went on to provide that if the boy married in breach of this condition the bequests would be void. It surely is not coincidental that the marriage contract of the boy with Arabella has her father contributing (Surprise! Surprise!) £5,000. Obviously, Arabella met the test because the boy did inherit. Parents played rough in those days and as I said, James I was a control freak.[69]

Arabella and James II were living at least part of the time at Northwick and had a son also called James–James III–in 1701. James II and Arabella both died in 1705.

James II's estate was inventoried in December 1705 in wonderful detail. The principal ground floor rooms in the house were a Great Parlour (which seems to have been unfinished as the inventory includes a "dore case frame intended for the Great Parlour" and furniture in other rooms is said to belong in the Great Parlour which almost must have been a big room in the filled in U behind the splendid new façade), "a Little Parlour, a Hall, Great Stayres with a little bedroom under them, an Old Diningroom and Sir James Closet (*i.e.* a den or study)". The principal bedrooms seem to have been on the first floor with other bedrooms in the "Garets". The house was fully stocked with large quantities of itemized personal property. Interestingly there is no mention of the large (6' x 10') family picture of John I's family, which was in the house in the 19th century. That, and the fact that the "Great Parlour" was not quite complete, suggests that the young family was still principally at Harrow though James I had a house in London as well. Clearly the family was also living at Northwick as there were a coach stable with

---

[68] Rushout genealogy is a nightmare. The names James, John, George and Elizabeth appear again and again. That's not too bad but when one son named James dies, his next-born little brother gets called James too. In the 18th century we get to play the "Which Elizabeth?" game as we are spoiled for choice. James I also had the following children: William Rushout born October 9, 1670 at 5 a.m. baptized same morning but died young; Alice born at Montpellier June 4, 1672 at 5 a.m. and baptized the same day (married October 14, 1694 to Edward Sandys, had a daughter Alice in October 1696); Catherine born April 18, 1676 (married December 31, 1696 to Samual Pitt). Catherine had a son Edmund on December 4, 1695 and a daughter Alice born October 22, 1696 but she died eight days later. Then Catherine had a son Samuel in 1697; James II born July 12, 1677; another William born January 5, 1679 (Julian) died December 13, 1679; Jane born February 21, 1681 (Julian) died May 6, 1690, buried at Blockley; Elizabeth born February 20, 1682 at Northwick, baptized on the 22nd at Blockley; John III born February 6, 1685; and George born July 16, 1688.

[69] James I seems to have been a pretty nasty piece of work in general. Bits of his correspondence remain in the Worcester Records Office and suggest that he was haughty and a bully, but I suggest his will alone would prove that.

six black coach horses, a cart stable housing "four old cart horses", "Coach Houses" [sic] with a coach and "very old chariot", and numerous out-houses including the greenhouse with thirty orange trees in tubs, a pomegranate tree, a bay tree, and six "laurestines" (a laurel tree?) and five "figgtrees" all in tubs and a like number of plants in pots. Clearly the greenhouse was up and thriving by 1705; it must be contemporaneous with the west façade. It has been suggested by various commentators that it was re-built later because the stonework is so crisp but I don't see that as compelling. However, a drawing dated 1819 in the Worcester Records Office suggests that it then had two extensions on the south front but these are not there now and are not indicated on a 1778 plan by Walter Emes nor on a 1783 print showing a glimpse of the greenhouse. The greenhouse has, however, been much altered over the years. The north side is relatively new. There is evidence of a smaller building being appended to it on the east and old drawings show possibly ancillary buildings which have long since disappeared.

There are lead gutter leads on the west façade with the date 1686 and the initials IR for Iacobus Rushout, but those are not original and James never used the Latin form of his name. The arms carved on the west pediment are the best evidence of who built it.

The west pediment

Two arms are impaled (*i.e.,* placed side by side, each on one half of the shield) and the side on the left (as you view it) includes the two lions passant-guardant which are in the fictitious Rushout French pedigree from 1652 and eventually show up in the arms of the 3rd Baron in *Burke's Peerage*. The other side is the arms of the Pitt family–James' wife. The arms are over-the-top figuratively as well as literally with a motto, mantling (draping fabric) and a crest, all of which seems a bit much for a Baronet. I wonder how James felt about putting this pretentious fiction into stone along with the symbol of his purchased baronetcy? The motto reads "Dulcis Saturat Ovies". The fiction of the ancient family motto of "Par Ternis Suppar" had not yet been invented. As for the one employed here, I cannot translate it or trace it, but since the root words are "charming, satisfying sheep" it may not bear looking into. As noted below, something more grand in mottos was to come.

On the death of their parents in 1705 the infant James III and his sister Elizabeth were removed from Northwick and almost all the servants were discharged with "their arrears of wages paid and an extra quarter in addition as it was unlikely they would gain re-employment until the spring".[70] A steward was kept on to guard the possessions left in the Mansion.

---

[70] Inventory, p. 308.

NORTHWICK GETS REMODELED AGAIN

James III died in 1711 and was succeeded in the Baronetcy and the estate of Northwick by his uncle John, John III, who was born in 1685[71], joined the Horse Guards as a cornet (the lowest grade of army officer–a rank held even by noble thirteen-year-olds) in 1705, became a captain in 1710 and retired from the army in 1712. He became a MP in 1713. He later found it politically useful to claim that he retired because the head of his regiment was "garbling the army with a view to defeat the Hanoverian Succession" (nice positioning that).

John Rushout, 3rd Baronet by Kneller, 1716.

John lived at Harrow until he married in 1729. Styles changed quite a lot and this is how he had himself portrayed in 1726.

John Rushout, artist unknown, 1726.

---

[71] John II was James I's second son, so upon the deaths of James II and James III, under James I's will almost everything moved over to John III, the second son and his sons.

John married Anne Compton, daughter of the 4th Earl of Northampton. John's sister, Elizabeth, had married the 4th Earl in 1726. The Earl died a year later; John married Anne, the Earl's daughter by the Earl's first wife in 1729, so his sister became his stepmother-in-law.

Anne Compton by Allan Ramsay, 1743, and Elizabeth Rushout by Francis Cotes, 1762.

This portrait of Anne is now in the National Trust Collection at Chirk Castle in Wales, and how it got there is very modestly interesting and of some later significance.

John and Anne had two children, John IV and Elizabeth. The above portrait of Elizabeth is also at Chirk Castle.[72]

John III was a self-promoter. The entry in *The English Baronetage, Volume III* entitled "Baronets Created by K. Charles II"[73] starts the entry for James I's baronetcy with "This family is said to be originally of English extraction, but long since went into France, and there settled; where we find (a) Thibaut Rouhaut, *Sieur de Boismenart,* from whom this house derives its descent; he lived in the year 1300..." The entry goes on to describe various descendants with terms such as "a valiant knight", "distinguished himself on several occasions", "great reputation", "much applauded", "considerable of figure", "mareschal of France", "governor of Paris", "recorded by French historians in their catalogue of illustrious persons", "highly signalized for his courage", *etc.* It then reports that "John, the youngest son of the mareschal de Gamaches, went into Flanders, where he settled" and "from whom in a direct male line, after several generations, was descended" our John I. Pretty impressive, what? All rubbish. All cited to "Ex. Inf. Dom. J. Rushout, Bar."

---

[72] Elizabeth was born in 1735 and married Richard Middelton who owned Chirk Castle. Elizabeth and Richard had a daughter named Charlotte Myddelton (born 1770) who married a man named Robert Biddulph in 1801, whereupon Robert changed the family name to Myddelton-Biddulph. Charlotte and Richard had three children, one of whom became General Thomas Myddelton-Biddulph (born 1809, died September 28, 1878). General Thomas had a son named Victor, born in 1860, who died on February 13, 1919. The significance of these developments is revealed on page 99 below.

[73] London, 1741, p. 304.

Is it possible that John III did not know that his family was rooted in Flanders from at least 1382 and that his great-great-grandfather was living in Izegem in the mid-16th century? He certainly knew that his precious baronetcy was purchased for cash for his father. John III was on the make, married to the daughter of an Earl and questing for a peerage. He probably felt he needed credentials to go with the fancy country estate. The invention of English origin is a particularly nice touch in a period when England was periodically at war with France.

This urge to pursue the French connection did not end with John III. In 1845, two nieces of the second baron contacted a M. Darsy who was a Notary and member of the Antiquarian Society of Picardy who wrote a report on "this branch of your family" It seems the ladies (who are not identified, but the only nieces of the second baron living in 1845 were Harriet and Georgina) had visited ruins in Gamaches and solicited this report to please their uncle. It rehashes the Rouhault genealogy again without actually linking that family to John I. Why were they still picking at this bone one hundred years after John III made his claims? Why, indeed, had it been so important to John I?

John III gives us the first example we have of intra-familial squabbles over money in the Rushout line. Primogenture created the need to leave some provision for the widow and younger children. While widows often had rights under their marriage contracts to lifelong protection, it was natural to leave the rest with something.

James I's will was hideously complex, leaving contingent life estates and allowances for those who came after him. His son, James II, followed his father's pattern. Upon his marriage in 1699, anticipating that he might leave a widow and children with the first surviving male being the big winner, James II imposed a trust on three of his many properties and provided that those properties would provide a £5,000 lump sum and a £100-per-year allowance to be shared among his daughters if his male heirs did not survive him. The idea was that since the bulk of his estate would go elsewhere in James I's male line if James II did not have male survivors, James II's daughters should get something. If, on the other hand, James II did have male survivors, presumably the winner would do something for the females.

In 1705, James II's estate planning switched from the providential structuring by a bridegroom to the final thoughts of a dying man. His wife, Arabella, had died, and James II himself was so sick his will says he knows he had a marriage settlement with "my dearly beloved wife, now deceased, (the contents of which settlement I may have forgot, and by reason of my present illness cannot immediately refer to)". He knew he had a little boy, James III, and a little girl and in his will dated November 12, 1705, he made sure the little girl, Elizabeth, would get £5,000 outright on the earlier of her marriage or her 21st birthday. As an afterthought, on December 2, 1705, James II executed a codicil raising the £5,000 to £8,000 if James III should die leaving Elizabeth as sole survivor.

James III died on September 21, 1714. Elizabeth was still an infant, but someone acting on her behalf began a legal proceeding to establish her rights under her father's and her grandfather's will. Because her brother had died, she had also inherited the three properties from which her annual allowance had been paid and her £5,000 would be paid. In 1716, the court ruled that because of the quirk that Elizabeth inherited the three properties, her entitlement to

£5,000 from those properties was extinguished, but that when she was 21, she could still elect to take the £8,000 under her father's will.

When Elizabeth turned 21 and wanted the £8,000, James III appealed from the 1716 ruling. James III's view was that Elizabeth was getting £800 every year from the three properties she inherited, so she should not get the £8,000, which would have to come out of his pocket. In 1725 the House of Lords affirmed that James III had to pay his niece the £8,000.

The National Archive suggests that a pound in 1720 would be worth about £85 in 2005, and that in 1720, a skilled craftsman would have to work about thirteen days to earn a pound. So Elizabeth's protectors and her uncle were squabbling over something like £680,000 and litigated for eleven years at what must have been horrendous expense. That is not small money. Some adult protector was fighting Elizabeth's corner rather aggressively and indeed along the way a special master had to be appointed to sort out all her claims so I can see how the litigation could have been fueled by animosities. But still, James III received a bundle. His brother, James II, on his deathbed wrote and revised a will to make sure that his daughter would be protected–though he remembered the trust if not its terms. That daughter, Elizabeth, got lucky and separately inherited the three valuable properties, the subject of the trust for her benefit. John III's argument seems to have boiled down to this: 'It ain't fair; she ended up getting plenty–more than my brother intended.' Yet by dumb luck in surviving his brother, his sister-in-law and his nephew, John III had plenty–more than he ever could have dreamed. But still he had to fight over money with his niece. John III was not a nice person, as we will see again later in reviewing his political career.

A Side Note on John III and the South Sea Company

This is yet another excursion without a particular destination–simply another illustration of how the Rushouts (John III in this case) were minor players in the ruling classes of their times and how so many of the players were connected by blood or marriage.

What initially caught my eye in this case was that Sir Thomas Vernon was a director of the South Sea Company from its founding in 1711 until 1715, and had been deeply involved in the creation of the Company. John II, John III's nephew, had married Sir Thomas' daughter, Arabella, in 1699, thus starting the Rushout/Vernon connection.

But first, a word on the South Sea Company. The Company was created to restructure the English national debt, and as conceived, was actually a very imaginative offering under which holders of illiquid Crown obligations, which were trading under par, could exchange them for Company shares, which promised a dividend indirectly guaranteed by the Crown. The dividends were lower than the interest rate on the exchanged obligations (this benefitting the Crown) but the shares were quite liquid and carried an equity kicker in a trading company which promised to be similar to the East India Company. Appendix IV is a fuller description of what is now called the South Sea Bubble, but suffice it to say that largely because of the connivance and outright fraud of insiders and government ministers and members of Parliament, a lot of the later investors in the Company lost a lot of money. It's actually a great story; I encourage you to at least glance through it.

Now coming to the point. Thomas Vernon was a wealthy Turkey merchant who became an MP in 1710. He was also the father-in-law of John Aislabie, a wily politician who became Treasurer of the Navy (a job that John III got and abused about fifty years later). Aislabie became Chancellor of the Exchequer and took bribes to promote the interests of the South Sea Company. He justly ended up in the Tower for a while, and unjustly, for his sins only forfeited £45,000 of his fortune, leaving him with £120,000. Vernon ceased to be a director of the Company in 1715 when, as a Tory, he was probably forced out in a political shift on the ascension of George I. Vernon was expelled from Parliament in 1721 on a finding that he had tried to influence Parliament's investigation into his son-in-law Aislabie's conduct.

John III was an MP from 1713 onwards and he was also a small shareholder in the South Sea Company at least as of December 25, 1714 (which is the only shareholder list I have found). He owned Company shares worth at least £1,000 par value (equal to about £76,000 in 2005) but there were about twelve hundred shareholders who held at least £1,000 par value in shares so at that point at least, John III was not a big player. Sir Isaac Newton is on the list holding at least £3,000 par value. I have found no evidence as to whether or when John III sold his shares advantageously and no evidence that he was caught up in the ensuing scandal; his name does not appear on the lists of officers and directors of the Company who were attainted in the parliamentary inquiries into the Company's affairs after the Bubble burst in 1720.

So thus far, all this shows yet again is how tightly knit the English moneyed and political classes were. We have seen, and will see again, how those connections could fray, especially in disputes about money such as John III's attempt to deprive his niece, Elizabeth (Sir Thomas' granddaughter) of £8,000. Another nice touch: as an MP, John III would have been obliged to vote on Sir Thomas' expulsion from Parliament.

AN EXTREME DIGRESSION ON ARISTOCRATIC IN-BREEDING

The higher level of English society has until very recently been very thinly populated and they all seemed to know each other and marry into each other's families. Were it not for the beneficial side effects of habitual adultery, the English upper class would be populated by driveling idiots (well, a lot more driveling idiots).

Fair warning: This section, which links to Northwick a portrait which we own, is possibly of interest only to about five close friends and relations. Well, remotely possibly. Many years ago, my wife Danielle and I bought a portrait of an English lady in late Elizabethan dress. One could say that this started the descent into, if not madness, then into the peculiarity of which the present work is merely symptomatic. We found out who the sitter was, we found and visited her home and we learned quite a lot about her and her family.

The sitter was Mary Heveningham who in 1599 married a man named James Pytts and went to live at a large estate in a remote corner of Worcestershire called Kyre Wyard which James' father, Edward Pytts, had acquired in 1576. Edward Pytts had an uncle, Thomas Pytts, who acquired the manor of Harrow-on-the-Hill; Thomas' descendant, Alice Pitts (as the name was more commonly spelled), married James Rushout thus beginning the Rushout connection with Harrow. Mary, the sitter in the portrait, had three children by James Pytts. Her son and heir, also named Edward, died childless (after years of litigating very nastily with his mother over property for years) and left Kyre to his cousin, Samuel Pytts, whose second wife was a young woman named Catherine Rushout, daughter of James I. Catherine died in 1702 at the age of 28, possibly consequent on the birth of her daughter also named Catherine. *The Kyre Park Charters* by John Amphett, printed for the Worcestershire Historical Society in 1901, found obscure, very local origins for Edward Pytts around Kyre as there are numerous references to people of a similar name in the manor records, but the author admits that Pytts was made a "filicer" (clerk of superior courts) of counties in 1563 at the age of 23 "and one cannot see where the influence necessary to obtain so lucrative a post for so young a man was so situated."[74] The Visitation of Worcestershire (a spot-check for imposters claiming the right to arms) in 1634 recorded the Pytts family history as including the progeny of one John Pytt who had two sons, one son had granddaughters, one of whom was Alice Pitt who married James Rushout and the other had a son who became Sir Edward Pytt "who purchased the manor of Kyre-Wyard in 1577."[75] Clearly the extended family made its fortune in the greater London area, not in Worcestershire.

Kyre, like Blockley, is in the Domesday book. Kyre and Northwick are on the Saxton and Speed maps of Worcestershire and have significant, traceable roots going back about one thousand years. Several years ago we discovered in the Kyre church adjacent to the remnants of the house where Mary had lived all her married life, a memorial to Catherine Rushout, daughter of James Rushout of Northwick Park. That was it; I was well and truly hooked. In the 17th century, Kyre and Northwick were on opposite sides of the middle of nowhere. Who were these

---

[74] Amphett, p. ix.

[75] *The Heraldry of Worcestershire, Volume II*, H. Sydney Grazebrook, London, 1873.

people and how did this connection occur? James Rushout married a Pitt of Harrow and his daughter married a Pytts of Kyre, the great grandson of Mary Pytts, the sitter in our most treasured portrait.

A footnote to this footnote: English testate and intestate succession is a jungle. Kyre passed out of the Rushout line early in the 18th century but in 1832, after yet another Pytts died childless and his surviving widow went to her reward, the estate reverted to the issue of Catherine Pytts, the little granddaughter of James I born in 1702. That family held Kyre until 1931 when they must have been financially ruined because they sold Kyre and all its contents–paneling, plumbing, everything including our favorite portrait which had hung in the house since it was painted in 1612.

Getting back to Northwick, perhaps on the occasion of his marriage John III began to remodel Northwick in the 1730s, using designs prepared by a well-known amateur architect, Lord Burlington. Burlington rebuilt the towers on the east façade, re-organized the front hall and replaced what had probably been stone mullioned windows of the Childe construction.

 As to the towers, the Historic Building Report on Northwick concludes that they are early 17th-century but if that be true then it seems that they were totally re-clad in the 18th century. All the detail is much crisper than on the 1686 west façade to the point that differential weathering cannot account for it. It seems reasonable to infer that stone mullion windows were taken out of the house at one point and that someone, probably Burlington, in the 1730s, added some decorative details to the east façade. The towers really are quite anomalous and have nothing to do with what must have been a 17th-century façade with Dutch gables. They have no apparent purpose. They are just 'there'. Maybe the kindest thing one could say is that Burlington found them there and re-clad them making the best of a bad job. The rainspout on the revised east façade dates its completion to 1732.

One amusing note: James I placed his arms impaled with Pitt in the pediment of the west façade. Marrying the daughter of an Earl was clearly a step up for John III who impaled his arms with those of his Northampton wife on the east façade.

The east façade

The next architectural intervention seems to have been by John Woolfe in the mid-18th century. At some point after Burlington finished (c. 1730) and before Walter Emes did a drawing of the complex with a view to planning alterations "immediately about the house at Northwick", the whole south façade was replaced with the bow windows added up to the second story.

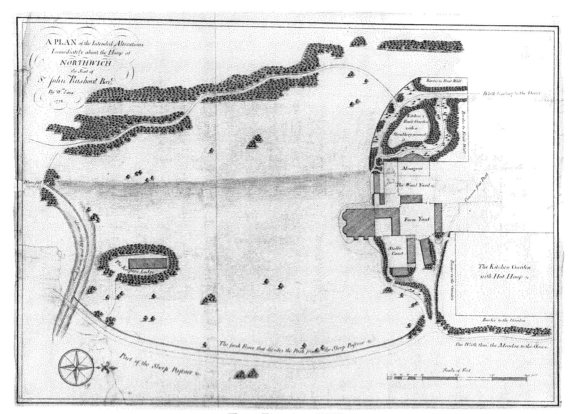

Emes Drawing, 1778

Two views by Anne Rushout, circa 1805

We know from the drawings above by Anne Rushout, John IV's daughter, that there was a doorway between the two bows and the bows were originally two stories high.

It seems likely that John III improved the park around Northwick. There is a lovely print dated 1783 showing four people in a deer park near the lake enjoying a view of the Mansion.

It also shows carriage drives around the lake. The craze for having hundreds of men work for years to alter landscape originated in the mid-18th century with "Capability" Brown, who did similar work for Alan Bathhurst at Cirencester and perhaps for the Pytts at Kyre. Northwick's landscape is probably predominantly the work of William Emes, as he specialized in creating lakes in flat landscapes.

The 1783 view by James Ross

John V had this large map made of the whole estate in 1819.

Two details in the large map are interesting. The Mansion and outbuildings:

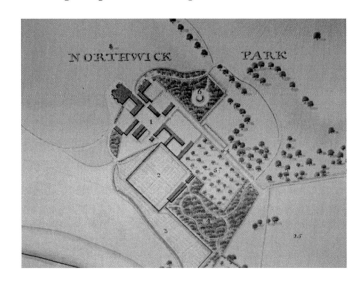

The Village of Blockley:

John III considerably enlarged the estate, first under an enclosure act of 1733 which gave him control of land that he had leased around the village of Blockley and then, upon the enclosure of the rest of the parish in 1773, when he got 60% of the land awarded. See Appendix II for a brief introduction to the Enclosure. John III died in 1775.

WHO ELSE LIVED AT NORTHWICK?

John IV, born July 23, 1738, married Rebecca Bowles, "the beauty of Essex", daughter of Humphry Bowles, a wealthy glassmaker who was also a part-time merchant with an office in London.

A digression is in order at this point because two properties come into the Rushout family here. In 1748, Humphry Bowles acquired an estate on the Welsh border called Burford House (near Tenbury).[76] Then, in 1759, he purchased 60 acres and a 17th-century house called Wanstead Grove in Essex within Epping Forest. These properties will feature below.

Rebecca was rich and beautiful. Among the many portraits of her is one below with her daughter Anne by Angelica Kauffman.

Rebecca and Anne after Angelica Kauffman.

Rebecca is also said to be in a family group by Zoffany, which I have been unable to locate.

---

[76] Burford House is a lovely place. St Mary's Church, which is adjacent to the house, is an important church with some equally important monuments and paintings, as well as some less important and undistinguished memorials to Rushouts. Giving credit where credit is indeed due, the Rushouts and Bowles preserved the place without the awful Victorian restoration that so many great churches suffered. Another bit of luck is that Burford House and its garden have been preserved. The house is a 17th-century shell with an 18th-century interior which some commercial enterprise has acquired and uses to sell upscale home decoration as part of a large garden centre that they run as an adjunct to the original gardens–the discretion of these entrepreneurs is a rarely-seen view of the acceptable face of capitalism.

Rebecca and John had three daughters, each quite pretty. The miniature of the three girls (below) by Andrew Plimer, now in the Huntington Library in California, was engraved and widely sold as *The Three Graces*.

A few words about the girls: Anne, the oldest (in the center in the Plimer miniature above) was like her mother–beautiful and talented. An individual miniature of Anne by Plimer appears on the next page.

Anne Rushout by Plimer, circa 1800.

Born in 1767, she grew up at Northwick. You get the feeling it was a happy childhood. She assembled a commonplace book, a compendium of household hints, which is in the Worcester Records Office, and a sort of a guest book, which is in the University of London Library–the latter being filled with notes left by guests at Northwick including two by Warren Hastings. She was a modestly competent but pleasing watercolorist. Six of her views of Northwick were engraved and privately printed in 1815. Two of those were reproduced earlier in this text. Four of her watercolors of Wanstead showed up recently behind a picture in an old frame and ended up in the Redbridge Museum in Ilford. A few of her Northwick paintings are in the private collection of Jack Baggott, antiques dealer at Stow. She also painted china with images of Northwick (a very lady-like hobby of the early 19th century).[77]

The tragedy of Anne's life was that she was engaged to marry her cousin, William Sidney Bowles, and at the last minute William Sidney threw her over and married her younger sister, Elizabeth (on the left in the Plimer). This caused serious strains in the family. Though there was a marriage settlement and the couple was married at St George's, Hanover Square, close to Lord Northwick's townhouse at 7 Park St and thus got the minimum standard recognition, they promptly decamped for Rome where the groom died in 1806 and was buried in the English cemetery. Anne died owning a locket with William Sidney's hair in it. She never married.

---

[77] Courtesy of John Haggart.

As it happened, Humphry Bowles' estate at Wanstead Grove was inherited by his son George who was also an art collector. George not only collected art but he seems to have collected an artist as well. He collected or commissioned at least forty-nine works by Angelica Kauffman including the famous picture of his sister Rebecca and Anne. As the family biographer observes, at that time the works of Gainsborough, Romney and Reynolds were to be had for almost the same, perhaps less money. "It must be owned that the descendants of Angelica's admirers have some cause to grumble."[78] (Angelica similarly ensnared and lumbered three other wealthy men–definitely a close following.) Her self-portrait suggests her appeal.

Anne inherited a life estate in Wanstead Grove as well as her uncle's house in Cavendish Square and a lot of money when her uncle George died in 1817. When her mother died in 1818, she renovated Wanstead Grove at the extraordinary cost of £10,000, unfortunately disposing of much of the 17th- and early 18th-century furniture as "old fashioned". She lived at Wanstead until her death in 1849.[79]

John IV was created Baron Northwick of Northwick Park, taking his seat in the House of Lords on April 11, 1799 and he died October 20, 1800.[80]

Angelica Kauffman's self-portrait, circa 1780.

---

[78] Bowles, p. 97.

[79] Some of her diaries are in the University Library, London. They start in 1826 and, sadly, they progress into what seems to be a disintegration of her personality. This beautiful, talented, French-speaking lady becomes a religious obsessive, seeming at first to make detailed notes of sermons by others which she indexes and underscores and then seeming to write her own. By the 1830s this daughter and sister of peers is going to chapel (Methodist or Baptist–middle and lower class) twice a day and can write of nothing else.

[80] John IV was a beneficiary of the second Blockley enclosure in 1799 receiving the 72½-acre Sedcumb farm bordering on Broad Campden, plus an additional 89 acres on Broad Campden Hill. (J.P. Nelson, *Broad Campden*, privately printed, 1970).

THE RUSHOUTS IN PARLIAMENT

Putting the Rushouts' political careers in context without overwhelming this little text requires a very light touch.

English politics in the 17th and 18th centuries was quite different from that of the late 20th century simply because the King actually ruled, albeit requiring the support of Parliament. The Parliamentary electoral process in the 18th century was so different from anything we would recognize that it deserves a few words of explanation. For one thing, peers were members of Commons; the Dukes of Devonshire sat in succession through the period, as did representatives of almost all the great aristocratic families.

Strange rules governing apportionment and qualification of electors had developed in earlier centuries but through the period, there were about five hundred constituencies, most in England and few in Wales and Scotland.

The constituencies overlapped. Each of the forty English counties elected two members with the voters all meeting property holding qualifications. Though the basic qualification was owning property subject to a land tax of 40 shillings per year, you could also qualify as the owner of leaseholds, ecclesiastical benefices and appointments in Government service—all in some sense men with considerable assured incomes. Candidates for the counties tended to be selected by leading peers and country gentlemen but then straw polls were held among electors and if a selected candidate looked to be a loser, they withdrew rather than go to the trouble and expense of running. James I sat for Worcestershire after the election of 1689 having been hand-picked for the seat by the King's agents who were looking for "sound" candidates to support.

About four hundred members were returned from towns and cities—boroughs—with about half selecting two members and larger ones, such as London, selecting as many as four. Qualification to vote varied widely among the boroughs. A small handful allowed all inhabitant householders to vote. Many of those elections were simply bought for cash or drink, or dictated by the landlord who controlled the way his tenants voted.

About one hundred boroughs gave the franchise to "freemen"—a vague term that tended to mean membership in one of the livery companies (guilds) or membership in the family of such a member. Because the status of being a freeman tended to be controlled by the municipal corporations (recipients of royal charters) which controlled and administered the boroughs and which in turn tended to be controlled by a handful of representatives of the leading interests and families, the size and character of the electorate of freemen could be tightly controlled. In short, you had to be a member of the 'club' to vote and the Corporations controlled club membership.

In another thirty or so boroughs, the Corporation itself designated the member, and as the Corporations were often controlled by local patrons, the results tended to follow the wishes of a handful of people. Because the King granted the corporate charter and dictated its terms, he could confine the franchise to a few people whom he hoped to influence. The Rushouts stood for Evesham which was technically corporate because under the second charter of Evesham granted by James I, representatives were to be chosen by "the mayor, aldermen and burgesses" of the borough. "Burgess" was the local equivalent of "freeman." Early in the century the charter was construed as limiting the vote to "capital freemen" who were the five or so richest but later it was construed to mean all freemen so the franchise was extended *de facto*. These elections were occasionally contested–sometimes bitterly. James I lost his seat in Evesham in 1694 due to what he called "foul practices." In 1780, one candidate elected with John IV sent a carriage to London to transport one non-resident freeman back to Evesham to vote in a close election. John III stood for Malmesbury, a Corporate seat, from 1712-1722. As mayor of Malmesbury, he could, in effect, nominate himself. He then stood for Malmesbury and Evesham simultaneously in 1722, was elected in both, but unseated in Malmesbury in a post-election contest so he served for Evesham until 1768.

In about thirty boroughs, only those who paid the poor tax (called "scot and lot")[81] had the right to vote so the underclass was excluded. These voters were commonly open to bribery and some were controlled by local magnates and landlords.

The strangest qualification to vote was "burgage" in which by tradition, the right to vote passed with title to a specific bit of land–so if you owned enough of those parcels in the borough, you controlled the election. You could sell your seat by selling the properties. These tended to become the "rotten boroughs." There were about thirty burgage boroughs only one of which had genuine elections because the burgages were widely held.

Oxford and Cambridge universities each elected two members with the electorate confined to doctors and masters of arts.

Thus, the phrase "all politics is local politics" is particularly apt to describe 18th-century England. The King was in a position of power because he paid for the civil and foreign service and controlled all appointments right down to local revenue collection including appointments in the army and navy. Very importantly, the King distributed all honors and most positions with a potential for profit. The King used the power of patronage to secure the loyalty or compliance of members of Parliament and indeed had a small fund he could use to pay election expenses of his favorites in key contested elections.

The King's task was to pick individuals as ministers who could corral enough votes to support the King's policies and wishes. A leader's tenure as a minister ended when he could no longer muster the support necessary to pass the King's agenda. Most of the ministers were peers many of whom had their own power bases through ownership of vast properties where they as lord controlled the vote.

The Rushouts' political careers occurred in this context:

Charles II was a clever, dissolute cynic. What Charles II introduced was endemic corruption. Charles' view was that all men and women were whores and all that differed among them is their prices. His Privy Council developed bribery as a fine art as a way of securing votes. His courtiers became incredibly wealthy. Salaries and pensions for the favored or pliable were huge. James II was so arbitrary and pro-Catholic that he was forced out in 1688 in favor of his

---

[81] From the Old French *escot* and Old English *sceot,* meaning "payment". Those who avoided paying this tax "got off scot-free".

daughter Mary II and her Dutch Protestant husband who became William III. To secure a Protestant succession in perpetuity and exclude re-entry by James II's Catholic son who styled himself James III, the Act of Settlement was passed in 1701 once it became highly unlikely Queen Anne would have an heir. That statute designated a Protestant granddaughter of James I and her Protestant descendants who had not married a Catholic as the successors to Anne. That woman was married to the head of a duchy in the north of Germany, which is called the House of Hanover after its principal city. When Anne died childless in 1714, a Hanoverian became George I of Great Britain.

My sense of these developments is that while a desire to suppress religious conflict by mandating Protestantism was a large factor, the real drive was to move to a constitutional monarchy in which Parliament had the upper hand because its hand was on the purse. Though British politics after 1688 was also influenced by a sideshow movement to restore the Stuarts, that was never a really serious threat; it was used as a bogeyman to generate support for Protestant successors and to suppress unconditional royalists. None of the Stuarts even wanted to learn the trick of getting along with Parliament and as late as King James II tried to rule in defiance of Parliament, calling Parliament only when there was no alternative source of money.

Parliament through this period was a kaleidoscope of factions whose members had proclivities and interests, not disciplined party affiliations. The labels Tory and Whig existed in the 17th century but they did not define much except perhaps a tendency toward royal dominance for the Tories and a tendency toward Parliamentary dominance by the Whigs. The Tories were marginalized in the 18th century in large part because they were tarred with the brush of Jacobitism–favoring the restoration of the Stuarts by force. That for most of the 18th century politics was fought out between government Whigs and opposition Whigs tells the story of party affiliation.

This flux was further complicated by dynastic craziness in the House of Hanover. King George I could not abide his son and heir; the feeling was mutual. The son became George II and repeated the mutual loathing with his son Frederick, Prince of Wales. Frederick's mother, Queen Caroline, reportedly described her "dear first born" as the greatest ass, liar, canaille, and beast in the world and wished "most heartedly" that he was out of it. On her deathbed she reportedly said that a benefit of dying was that she would never see Frederick ("that monster") again. Frederick died before reaching the throne but his son, who became George III, was soon at loggerheads with his grandfather George II. Though it is beyond our period, George III was in a well-justified permanent rage at his son who ruled as George IV but had no heir so the pattern of inter-generational loathing ended with him. This hundred-year family soap opera had political significance because Princes of Wales have small but independent power bases based on their income from the Duchy of Cornwall which funded patronage and also allowed them to influence Parliamentary elections in Devon and Cornwall. The Princes could and repeatedly did organize opposition to their fathers' governments.

It was George I who found a way of herding the parliamentary cats. He came to rely on one member of Parliament, Robert Walpole, who in turn developed a patronage system to assemble the votes needed in Parliament to implement policies favored by the Crown. Walpole was at once the King's man in Parliament and a member of the King's Privy Council. The role that Walpole played evolved into what we would recognize as a prime minister but in the 18th century there was no one with that title and no chief minister or "Leader of the Commons" emerged from a defined, disciplined political party.

Until the 17th century the House of Commons was never truly representative of the general population and representation was never proportional. There was a reapportionment after the Civil War as the royalists turned the tables on the repudiated Puritans but still the members were generally nobles, greater and lesser gentry, merchants, shopkeepers, clergy and military officers.

So where did the Rushouts fit into this picture? They were fairly typical of the country gentlemen who dominated Parliament. The gentry's predominant characteristics were considerable land-based wealth, conservatism and independence. They felt a genuine duty to support the King and country but reserved the right to evaluate policies one by one, not as partisans but as men of good judgment. In particular, they carved out a role of watching over the government administrators with a view to preserving liberty and weeding out fraud and abuse. They tended to eschew political office both because they did not want to make the compromises necessary to obtain office and because they had more pressing local and personal interests to attend to. They tended to be armigerous and high church, rarely low church or dissenters. The Rushouts were almost perfect examples of this type except that, on the whole, they were even less active in Parliament than many of the gentry and were very much more interested in securing badges of honor.

James II served intermittently for Evesham followed after a gap by his son James III who served one term in 1701-03. Neither made a mark and both attended rarely.

John III served for Malmesbury from 1713-1722 and then for Evesham from 1722-1768 and was modestly active. The highlights in his Parliamentary career were:

• In June 1716 he voted against the Septennial Bill, which increased the maximum length of a Parliament (and thus the interval between general elections) from three to seven years. Extending the length tended to increase the power of the Whigs.

• In 1718 he voted against repeal of the Schism Act, which had required tutors and school masters to be Church of England communicants—a measure to suppress dissenters' schools.

• In 1719 he voted against the repeal of the Occasional Conformity Act, which barred Roman Catholics and non-conformists from occasionally taking communion in the Church of England so as to be eligible for public office.

• He initiated the inquiry into the Atterbury Plot in 1721. Lord Atterbury was a rabid high Anglican clergyman who became a Jacobite and eventually was accused of involvement in a plot to capture the family of George I and install James III. Though not convicted, he was banished from England for life.

• He sponsored the complaint leading to Lord Macclesfield's impeachment, of which he was a manager. Lord Macclesfield was a Whig politician who served as regent for George

I between Anne's death in 1714 and 1718 because George I could not speak English. He became Lord Chancellor in 1718 and was made an earl by his friend George I. He was impeached in 1725 for accepting more than £100,000 in bribes (about $11,000,000 today) and was unanimously convicted in the House of Lords.

• He also introduced a bill against election bribing, which passed in the Commons but was defeated in the Lords.

• He was a friend of William Pulteney. Pulteney was initially a strong supporter of Robert Walpole and became Secretary of War between 1714 and 1717 and a privy counselor but eventually fell out with Walpole whom he accused of being corrupt and tyrannical. Pulteney led the opposition to Walpole for years and when Walpole fell in 1741, Pulteney became a cabinet member in the Pelham government and acquired a peerage as Earl of Bath. When Pelham fell in 1746, Pulteney tried and failed to form a government.

• In 1727, he led an attack on Robert Walpole and thereafter remained in opposition as a chief supporter for Pulteney (for whom he acted as a second in Pulteney's 1731 duel with Lord Hervey). (Walpole called him "short of stature and choleric"; Horace Walpole called him "Old Dishcloth.")

• He supported an increased allowance for Frederick, Prince of Wales in 1737, by which time Frederick was in opposition to his father George II.

• When Walpole fell, Rushout became one of Pulteney's opposition representatives on the Treasury Board where he was in opposition to the first lord of the treasury, Wilmington. His opposition was bought off by a lucrative appointment as Treasurer of the Navy but he was forced out after a year when Pulteney lost power. Rushout had hopes for a peerage when Frederick came to the throne but Frederick died in 1751. So with Pulteney's death in 1764, Rushout attached himself to Newcastle, a long serving member of the house who was almost constantly a minister by reason of his close connection to George II and George III.

Rushout did nothing of note in his remaining years as a member other than to become Father of the House of Commons as the longest consecutively sitting member.

As to John III's career in Parliament: "He was a frequent and boring speaker, with a trick of always putting out one leg and looking at it while speaking".[82] He was appointed Lord of the Treasury but at the opening of the next session of Parliament, he

> "actually forgot he was lord of the Treasury. He got up to speak and when he came to the point of Hessian and Hanoverian troops was against 'em, and went so far as to say he saw as little occasion for them this year as there was in the last [thus going against the policy of the government of which he was a member]. [Other members] stared

---

[82] *The History of Parliament, The House of Commons, 1715-54*, Romney Sedgwick, ed. HMSO, pp. 395-96.

him in the face, which put him in mind who he was, so he said the heat of the House overcame him, and so sat down."

When he was forced out as Treasurer of the Navy, he "revenged himself for his dismissal by refusing to make any payments from the sums standing to his account as treasurer of the navy, thus putting a stop for 8 or 9 months to the payment of all seamen who had not received their pay up to the date of his dismissal." "His sole ambition was a peerage" which never came. He actually wrote to the Prime Minister in 1756 asking for a peerage but eventually received a curt reply that though four names were suggested to the King, the King thought three were enough.

His son, John IV, first stood for Evesham in 1761 with him and they were both elected.

The highlights of John IV's career were:

• He initially tended to be in opposition. In 1767 and 1770 he voted against the government in the matter of John Wilkes, an English radical with a checkered personal history who made history asserting the right of voters to select their representatives.

• He spoke against the Royal Marriages Act of 1772, which made it very difficult for anyone in the royal succession to marry without the consent of the King. As late as 1782, he was in opposition to Lord North who lost the first vote of no confidence in English history over his handling of the American Revolution.

• He voted for Fox's East India Bill of 1783, which would have taken control of India from the East India Company and lodged it with seven commissioners. The proponents of the bill, primarily Charles Fox and Edmund Burke, wanted the East India Company out of the political role of India (which the company enforced with its own armies) and confined to trading.

• Initially he supported the government's tough stand on America's demands leading to the revolution. He voted in favor of the Boston Port Act of 1773, which closed the port of Boston to all trade until the customs duty on the tea dumped by the "Tea Party" was paid and the East India Company was compensated for the destruction.

• However, in 1783 he voted in favor of Lord Shelborne's proposals to make peace with America on what were seen in England as very generous terms, as Shelborne wanted to foster favorable post-war economic and diplomatic ties with America.

• He supported Pitt in the Regency Crisis of 1789, which occurred when George III had a bout of his famous illness and the appointment of a regent was necessary. The Prince of Wales was to be the Regent but the issue was whether he would rule as if King or be under Parliament's thumb by requiring him to keep the King's present government (Pitt), have no right to create peers, no patronage rights, no power to grant pensions, no control over the King's person or real or personal estate. The King recovered on March 1, 1789 so the regency bill was moot but Rushout lost no time trying to leverage his support into a peerage applying for a peerage on April 27, 1789 and again in March 1790, July 21, 1794 and May 6, 1796. A year later, at George III's instance (not Pitt's) Rushout got his reward.

Rushout's finally successful appeal for a peerage and George III's response are fascinating. Rushout wrote to the King (the letter is undated):

"I had some years ago the honor of applying to your Majesty for a Peerage which was intended for my grandfather, when your Majesty was pleased to say my request should be considered. Since that time, fearful of being personally intrusive, I solicited the same favor through your Majesty's Minister, whose answer having flattered me with that success at some future period, which political arrangements then made inconvenient, I beg your Majesty's permission, now, once more to lay the ground of my solicitation before you.

My grandfather Sir James Rushout raised a Regiment for the support of King William and was one of the first, and most loyal commoners in Worcestershire, which county he represented, and resigned his seat in Parliament on being appointed his Majesty's Ambassador to Constantinople. He was to have been created a Peer before he left England and the Patent was making out [sic] when by a sudden and unexpected death he was deprived of the honours intended him.

My Father was so well known to your Majesty that it is needless for me to say more on that subject than that the late Prince of Wales condescended to treat him with great regard and friendship, and that he promised him a Peerage whenever it should be in his power to confer that honor. Some time after, when my Father lay dangerously ill, and it was apprehended his complaint might prove fatal, his Royal Highness was graciously pleased to send Sir George Lee to assure him, that in case of his death, his Royal Highness would certainly confer the same honor on me. In consequence of the friendship with which his Royal Highness honored my Father, I was introduced to your Majesty at a very early period of life, my conduct since that time, has I hope proved the warmth of my zeal and attachment to your Majesty's person.

Ever solicitous of obtaining an honor to which my fortune and situation in life I hope may justify my aspiring; it would be particularly gratifying to me to owe that high honor to your Majesty's goodness, at a moment, when I have the mortification and regret of feeling, that all my efforts have been unsuccessful, against the means used to deprive me of a borough, which has been represented by my family for a century past.

Should your Majesty condescend to grant me the honor I solicit, you will confer the highest obligation on me and my family; permit me Sir to add, that the most flattering circumstance attendant on success will be to owe it to your Majesty's goodness, which will ever be acknowledged with the greatest respect and gratitude by [*etc.*]"[83]

The King to William Pitt: [Kew, 26 July 1797.] "When Mr. Pitt mentioned the list of Peerages and his wish to be authorized by me on this promotion to declare that he is not at liberty to bring any fresh applications on that subject, it did not occur to me that he had omitted the name of a respectable Baronet whom he was authorized on the former promotion to acquaint in my name should be thought of the next occasion; I mean Sir John Rushout. Now, though I am sorry the number is so great, I think it better to add him on the present occasion as his disappointment would be [well] founded after what was said to him, and his pretensions are better than those of some of those proposed."[84]

Returning now to John V, by 1818 he has title to and possession of his seat. The first evidence of change to Northwick seems to have ensued from a fire in 1828 which caused the central staircase to be rebuilt, and perhaps at this time the bows were raised to the third story (they show in Victorian photographs).

The dramatic change, however, comes in 1832 with the addition of the Gallery to house the 2nd Baron's burgeoning art collection.

The Gallery

[83] Chatham Papers, 174. *The Later Correspondence of George III, Volume II,* Arthur Aspinall ed. Cambridge University Press, 1966, p. 495.

[84] Ibid, p. 603.

Even that did not suffice so said Baron (John V) built a large house in Cheltenham called Thirlestane House (now part of Cheltenham College) which housed the better bits of his collection and seems to have become his principal country residence–Cheltenham was a very social town, a place to see and be seen.

John V continued to travel and collect assiduously. Some of his diaries from the 1850s are at the University of London Library (mis-catalogued as being Anne's) and they continue his pattern of brief notes of where he had been and what he had seen without editorializing or revealing much.

Lord John's residuary estate totaled £133,537 but that is misleading because valuable property passed through other mechanisms.[85] His holdings included 4,215 acres in Worcestershire, 2,095 acres in Shropshire, 1,885 acres in Rutland, 1,260 acres in Middlesex, 365 acres in Gloucestershire, 88 acres in Wiltshire and 6 acres in Herefordshire, the total said to produce an income of £17,725 per year.[86]

The 3rd Baron, Lord George (John V's nephew), followed family traditions: he started as a coronet and retired as captain in the First Life Guards in 1842, MP for Evesham 1837-41 and for East Worcestershire 1847-59, alumnus and Governor of the Harrow School. He seems to have been a solid citizen whose contributions to the community, in addition to the usual charity, included building a viaduct and improving the road over Campden Hill and building an entire sewage system in Blockley after an outbreak of cholera in 1854 which killed fourteen people in a single week. The contract for the sewage system was based on a £1,125 estimate, a lot of money then but less than 10% of Lord John's annual income.

George I also tidied the estate up a bit, building and re-building outbuildings. In 1864 he ripped down the stables (now called 3, 4, 5 The Coach House) and what is now called The Stables (but was then called the stables and the piggeries) and rebuilt them more or less in their present location. In the Emes drawing of 1778 the space between them is trapezoidal but it is now rectangular. The drawings and specifications in the Worcester Records Office called for the existing structures to be removed and rebuilt in sections. Lord George also built a little extension to the coach house, which was a sort of garage but became our little house.

---

[85] For instance, Rebecca's will passed on heirlooms at Northwick with the house which was always entailed. "Heirlooms" seems to have had a broader scope at this time than the textbook definition of equipment necessary to operate inherited real property–the value of the Northwick heirlooms in Rebecca's will was set at £4,354 which is a huge sum. I suspect the family pictures were in that category.

[86] *Burke's Peerage*, 1867.

"A Lady and her Children": Rebecca with Anne, Harriet and John, after Daniel Gardner, 1778.

Rebecca had already used over £3,000 of her own funds to extend the terms of leases from the Bishop, adding three lives to the term of one and two lives to another. Measuring the term of leases in lives was customary in the West Midlands. The Bishop was doing it in the 10th century. The possible tenants were named individuals, some of whom would usually be young children, in the hope of having a long term. Infant mortality was a serious threat so the named children were usually at least six years old. That this practice carried on for hundreds of years evidences the stability of society in the district–families stayed in one place and their members were known. By contrast, this practice created big problems in Ireland in the 19th century when the mass migration caused by the famine often made it impossible to know whether measuring lives were still in being. The price of these extensions measured by lives seems to have been by formulas or rules of thumb. If you wanted to add five lives, including some young ones, the price might equal six years' rent value but a three-life extension might cost one and a half years' rent. In any event it was an occasion to haggle and there is a lovely letter from the Bishop to Rebecca dated August 12, 1803 saying:

> "It is not easy for me to write long letters, much less to enter into all the particulars which have passed in this tedious negotiation about the Blockley leases. Your Ladyship will therefore have the goodness to excuse the liberty I take in referring to the enclosed letter of Mr. Hurd [the Bishop's steward] for an explanation of some things mentioned in your favor to me. I have only to add, that, the case your Ladyship thinks it material, I will consent to the words–<u>and trees likely to become timber</u>–being erased from the leases, but no other alteration whatsoever. I have the honour to be, Madam, Your obedient humble servant R. Worcester."

Rather importantly, Lord George purchased the fee interest in the Bishop's leases. I have not found the actual deed but found a document dated February 15, 1860 called "Valuation of Leasehold Properties Belonging to the Right Honorable Lord Northwick as Lessee under the Lord Bishop of Worcester" in which the valuer states that the fee interest plus the standing timber was worth a total of £19,905.0.0. This report concludes: "the lessee offers this sum for the Lord Bishop's interest therein. We recommend that the offer be accepted." The nineteen-page valuation opens:

> There is no correct Map of the property valued. The greater portion is free of Tithe rent charges, there is therefore no Map.
>
> There is an old Map made at the time of the Inclosure of the Parish in 1773 which shows most of the Leasehold and the quantities of the allotments agree with the Leases, but this map does not show the different parcels as they at present exist although in the outline it is correct.
>
> Lord Northwick has a map of the Parish made by Eliot in 1819.[87] We have taken a copy of it, not only are the fences very much altered since this was made, but we have proved by testing it at several points that it is incorrect.
>
> Under these circumstances as Lord Northwick is anxious to enter into an agreement for the enfranchisement without delay we propose to attach to this Valuation a tracing from Lord Northwick's map which will correctly show the boundaries of the land valued, and adopt the quantities from the Inclosure Map, which are the same as those given in the leases.
>
> An actual survey should then be made to provide a correct Map to put on the Deed of enfranchisement and an addition or reduction according as the quantities prove more or less can afterwards be made to the consideration money.

The valuers then go lease by lease. Most of them had been made by John V on December 9, 1848 for three lives: his own, that of George Rushout who became the 3rd Baron and was then aged 47, and that of Algernon St. George William Rushout Cockerell then aged 17. Typically the valuer took the annual rent, deducted for the costs of repairs and insurance to get a net annual value, multiplied that by 30 years and added the value of the standing timber. I have not found the deed or the map but my instinct is that the Bishop's total fee interest was conveyed. Indeed, the recommended purchase price of £19,905 was a tremendous amount of money in 1860.[88]

---

[87] See p. 78 above.

[88] The Valuation notes that the greater portion is free of title rent charge and it appears that as part of the same transaction, George I sold back to the Bishop his interest as Lessee in the tithes of corn and grain of the two Upton Wolds, Stapenhill, Blockley Warren, Blockley Park and Blockley Downs for £1,582. The Worcester Records Office contains a draft of this contract but not the final deed. It seems reasonable to infer, however, that the Bishop sold the freeholds and in a linked transaction re-established his rights to what were called the Great Tithes (see footnote 54 above).

At the age of fifty-nine, Lord George married Elizabeth Augusta Warburton, a widow by whom he sired one daughter who died in infancy. When Lord George died in 1887, the Rushout male line became extinct and the Barony and Baronetcy lapsed. Elizabeth Augusta became the life tenant of Burford House as well but never lived there; she stayed at Northwick, dying in 1911.

Burford house had become the home of George I's sister, Georgina, who appears to have been a remarkable woman. I have been able to learn very little about her but a book entitled *Our Adventures During the War of 1870* (London: Bentley, 1871) by two English nurses is dedicated "To the Honorable Georgiana [sic] Rushout, for whose generous aid and sympathy to relieve the sick and wounded in the late war, we owe a debt of gratitude." That, coupled with Georgina's never having made a claim against the second baron's estate, prompted me to look at her will, made and amended 1884-88. She starts with a bequest of £20,000 for the Burford Church of which her father was a the vicar and goes on with an extraordinarily detailed list of bequests down to £15 for a named kitchen maid. She left £750 in trust to give one shilling a week to the inmates of the Burford alms house plus a shilling a week "to the woman who cleans the rooms once a week for those who are most infirm." Initially she left the bulk of her estate to her brother, George I, but when he died she left it to his widow, Elizabeth Augusta, whom she also made trustee of the various trusts she left. She seems to have been genuinely happy to do that. Someone should take a good look at Georgina. They may also verify something that I can only suspect: Georgina may be the creator of some very accomplished watercolors with a special skill at precise architectural rendering. There are sketches in WRO 705:66/441/43 which are unattributed but are dated 1847 and 1848. There is no other likely suspect at that date. I bought a dozen sketches from a sketchbook with Anne Rushout's bookmark on it but the paintings are not Anne's style and indeed in some respects are well beyond Anne's skill level.

In any event: Anne died in 1849 and her later diaries reveal an infirm hand and an impaired mind. An easy guess: The spinster aunt, Anne, tutored the niece who was perhaps a family favorite being called "my dear little granddaughter Georgina Rushout" in her grandmother Rebecca's will. Georgina is worth researching.

After Elizabeth Augusta died, Burford House went to Lord George's grand-nephew, grandson of the Cockerells of Seizencote (if the name sounds familiar, you've read Pepys' *Diary*—these Cockerells are his relatives on his mother's side) who had changed his name to Rushout but the will was contested in a lawsuit that went to the House of Lords. The cost of the litigation ruined the Cockerell-Rushout in question who had to sell Seizencote thus extinguishing the Rushout property interests in and around Blockley.

WHO COLLECTED WHAT?

I have probably led you to believe that there were just two collectors at Northwick, but that is by no means clear. In Captain Churchill's sales there were well over a thousand books, some of considerable age and apparent value. A Book of the Hours made for Charles the Bold, Duke of Burgundy, sold for 28,000 guineas but who originally added it to the collection? The Captain? Lord John? Or someone else. Lord John was an active book collector as well as an art collector and it seems likely that he assembled the one hundred volumes of auction catalogues for sales that occurred between 1800 and 1848. We can confidently attribute the 150 or so bound picture sales catalogues between 1805 and 1849 to John V. But what are we to make of the 291 sales catalogues largely of paintings for auctions conducted between 1754 and 1817? They were all bound in six volumes. Maybe Lord John picked them up at the house sale of some other collector. But can we rule out the possibility that John IV or even John III collected them. Maybe some of the famous art collection was assembled not by John V but by his father (or mother) or his grandfather. It goes even further back than that. The Churchill sale included bound volumes of pamphlets and speeches that almost certainly started with John I in 1642. They include a bound volume of sermons by N. Hardy, who clearly was John I's favorite preacher and preached at the funeral of John's young son and namesake.

The scope of the family's interests as evidenced by the library was considerable. Someone collected and bound nine volumes of papers and pamphlets on American subjects and there are two bound volumes of pamphlets and papers bearing on the slavery issue (largely on the anti-side) between 1777 and 1805. There are an additional two hundred and ten bound volumes and pamphlets and speeches dated 1792-1808.

Perhaps most interesting is that the Churchill sales included sixty-six Indian miniatures, largely early Mughal. Who collected these pictures? Though John V clearly had a very good eye and loved beautiful things, I have thus far found nothing to connect him clearly to the acquisition of these paintings. Could there be an association with Warren Hastings?

Hastings was the Governor General of India between 1771 and 1784 and unlike most of his predecessor and successors as British colonial rulers, Hastings was fascinated by, and deeply self-educated about, Indian culture. He learned Hindi-Urdu (later called Hindustani), Urdu, Persian and Bengali. Hastings was charged with corruption on his return to England but acquitted after a ruinous trial in Parliament, which took 148 days over seven years to reach a verdict. The trial was hugely political and the current historical view seems to be that Hastings was indeed largely an innocent victim of vicious personal attacks on him, though he did accept a few presents which he thought were his due. The major purpose of the prosecution led by Edmund Burke was aimed at containing the activities of the East India Company, which was governing an empire in its own interest.

Be that as it may, Hastings was a family friend of the Rushouts and spent a lot of time at Northwick. His diary entries include rides at Northwick with John V and the Duke of Gloucester, a nephew of George III, and dinners with Rebecca and Anne. He made several entries in Anne's commonplace books in the late 18th century, and a table of his and this Reynolds portrait of him (now in the National Portrait Gallery) remained at Northwick until the Churchill sale.

Warren Hastings by Reynolds, circa 1766.

Rebecca corresponded with him for years and some of that correspondence is included in Appendix III to give you some insight into her interesting and appealing personality.

The miniatures were not sold in 1859 but they may have been included in the books and prints which were exempted from the settlement Lord George made with his aunt and cousin. The Reynolds portrait was not in the sale either but it might have been exempt as an heirloom.

Hastings rebuilt a mansion at Daylesford, about ten miles away from Northwick, and retired there after he was acquitted in 1795. Anne Rushout made at least two paintings of the house for him. Hastings was improvident and constantly in debt. A biographer states that he had to sell a collection of Mughal paintings and John V would have been a possible purchaser.[89] It could be that Lord John bought the Hastings table at a disposal sale which occurred in 1853 when Hastings' stepson vacated Daylesford but the sale catalogue description of the "Persian Drawings" do not match up with the descriptions in the 1965 sale catalogue including "Indian Miniatures". Lord John did collect pictures associated with his famous acquaintances including a large number of engravings of Emma Hamilton and John Wilson's *Battle of Trafalgar*. Could

---

[89] *Dawning of the Raj* by Jeremy Bernstein, Ivan R. Dee, 2000, p. 280. See also *Warren Hastings* by Keith Feiling, p. 374. I have spent hours in the British Library going through Hastings' diaries, correspondence and bills and accounts (the man threw nothing away) but have failed to find a reference to the sale of the miniatures.

John's father or mother have acquired them? Frankly, I tend to regard John IV, Lord John's father, as a pompous boob, but what if I am missing something? What if those picture auction catalogues were his or Rebecca's and they started the great collection? These seemingly very fine Indian and Persian paintings are not the detritus of a boob. Identifying the collector is an intriguing puzzle and might reveal a few bright bits I've missed.

THE END OF THE RUSHOUTS

Northwick passed to Captain Churchill, a grandson of Lord George's widow, Elizabeth Augusta, as had been agreed in the Marriage Settlement between Augusta and Lord George. The Captain's father had married Elizabeth Augusta's daughter by her first marriage, so that put the Captain in line of succession. Captain Churchill (who never married) was childless, but Lord George's will had anticipated such a possibility. Do you remember the name Myddelton-Biddulph? John III's daughter Elizabeth married a Myddelton and they had a daughter who married a Biddulph, whereupon in 1801 the name became the hyphenate. That couple had a son who became General Sir Thomas Myddelton, a much-appreciated courtier of Queen Victoria, who visited him daily as he lay dying in 1878. The General had started as a Cornet in the 1st Regiment of Life Guards in 1826; Lord George became a Cornet in the same regiment in 1833. They must have gotten on well because Lord George's ultimate residuary beneficiary for Northwick if the Captain died without descendants (as he did) was Victor Myddelton-Biddulph, the son of his fellow officer and remote cousin, the General. As it happens, Victor himself died childless on February 13, 1919 and left no will, but Northwick could have gone to one of his surviving relatives. Yet Captain Churchill seems to have survived all the Myddleton-Biddulphs, and so it came to pass that upon his death, Northwick was sold as directed by his will.

I have noted again and again how it seems that everyone in this saga knew or had connections to everyone else. Captain Churchill's sister married into the Bathurst family. A Bathurst became an Earl in the 18th century and created a five mile long walled park in Cirencester. One of James Rushout's habitual borrowers was Alan Bathurst, prominent in the Bathurst line, and Rushouts and Bathursts were social friends for years. Sarah Churchill, the politically active wife of the first Duke of Marlborough and intimate friend of Queen Anne was in correspondence with the 3rd Baronet Rushout on political issues and her descendant inherited Northwick. I used the phrase before but it fits again: These people were in each other's pockets and beds for hundreds of years. Churchill's residuary legatee was Peter Bathurst of that family. And it was not all lovey-dovey. Captain Churchill and his co-trustees of the Northwick estate had to consult counsel because Peter Bathurst was a spendthrift, had some sort of interest in the estate and seems to have threatened litigation to shake out more money after he lost his first distribution. They made a settlement. In 1914, Churchill sued Bathurst in High Court Chancery Division to determine what were heirlooms, which passed with the house under the will of George I, and what were not. At the end of it, it came down to a squabble over whether the drawings had been framed and were on the walls. In 1916 there was an order that the Captain could purchase some items for £525. This leads to a more general point: No one fights more ruthlessly or at closer quarters over money than the English upper and landed classes. Utterly remorseless and shameless. They spent fortunes on lawyers devising the ultimate in dead-hand control of their property in labyrinthine wills, trusts and marriage settlements of mind-boggling complexity which time and again caused (and still cause) great properties to pass like a ping-pong ball not just over the net but onto different tables just because the tables were made two hundred years earlier out of wood from the same tree.

WORLD WAR II

The American 6th Armored Division took over Northwick on February 22, 1944 as part of a group that had 341 tanks in and around Moreton-in-Marsh in preparation for D-Day. A lot of ordnance was stored around the park. Companies A, B and C of the 15th Tank Battalion camped in a 70-acre site to the north of the Mansion adjacent to the road to Broad Campden which was turned into an American field hospital anticipating D-Day casualties. On June 6, 1944, D-Day, a long hospital train arrived at Blockley station transferring patients from hospitals in the south of England to make room for anticipated D-Day casualties. By early July, the hospital was receiving casualties from France.

The camp itself consisted of a large number of Nissen huts (named for the Canadian engineer who designed them; Americans called the same sort of thing Quonset huts). These were arcs of corrugated asbestos bent like a croquet hoop and driven in the ground with masonry walls on either end. There were separate brick toilets and kitchens in clusters. There were also about twenty long brick buildings for more serious hospital business. All this was thrown up in six months with the first medical staff arriving on December 20, 1943.

The camp was taken over on June 1, 1944 by the International Red Cross, which had jurisdiction over all prisoners of war in England, and was used to treat German and Italian prisoners of war. There was a large POW camp on the A-424 close to its junction with the A-44 housing mainly prisoners from the North African campaigns.

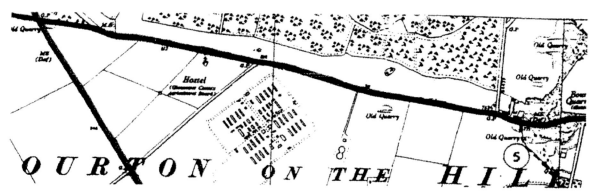

Ordnance survey of the POW camp

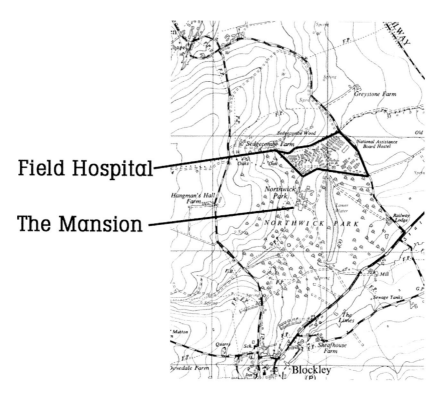

Field Hospital

The Mansion

The crosses are in the Polish corner of the Blockley cemetery.

After the war, the camp was abandoned but was taken over in 1947 to house Polish displaced persons. The Poles had escaped their homeland traveling to the east when Germany invaded. Eventually they were scattered all over the world and some ended up at Northwick from the Middle East, Africa, India and, of course, large numbers from Russia. By 1950, there were over eight hundred people living in the camp. Eventually the Nissen huts were divided into two sections and the brick structures were divided as well. The insides were eventually finished and painted and in pictures they looked like little holiday homes albeit with arching walls and ceilings. There developed a complete Polish community with schools, religious services, scout troops, and sports teams. In July 1952, General W. Anders, the leader of Free Poland, visited a rally of three thousand people at Northwick. Large numbers of Poles now lie in abandoned Polish sections of the cemeteries in Blockley and Chipping Campden.

There were more than a half a dozen similar camps for Polish refugees in England after the war and Northwick was among the last of them to close as it contained a lot of hard cases—people who couldn't make the transition to being economically self-supporting in England.

By the 1960s, the able people were moving out, and by 1968, the remaining few were transferred to camps in Devon and Wales and the Northwick camp closed. The huts and buildings were later converted for light industrial use, and while they certainly perform a useful function, basically nothing has been done to improve the place in sixty years and, overgrown with weeds, it looks like an industrial slum with no trace of the vibrant generation that was born and raised there nor of the soldiers, sailors and airmen who suffered and died there.[90]

---

[90] See: www.northwickparkpolishdpcamp.co.uk.

THE LATER YEARS

On Captain Spencer-Churchill's death, the estate was purchased by Michael Pearson, his grand-nephew, on behalf of Whitehall Securities, a subsidiary of S. Pearson and Co. Ltd., but the estate was let at a nominal rent as a drug rehabilitation center in 1967. Though the recovering addicts tried to fix the Mansion and outbuildings, a long process of neglect and decline was only momentarily abated. The founder of the drug rehab center describes what he found when he first went to Northwick in the late 1960s.

He must have entered through what is now called Burlington Court, an L-shaped structure which housed servants' quarters, the kitchen, *etc.* which also contained

> a long room with great metal hooks for hanging salted meat carcasses suspended from the beams. In some places a little light filtered in through holes in the roof, showing up rotten floor boards where rain had continually poured through…
>
> The house had in fact been completely empty for just three years, but the process of decay had started long before. Captain Spencer-Churchill had been an eccentric bachelor who lived almost exclusively for his valuable collections of art treasures, old coins and porcelains which he housed in a gallery which formed an extra wing to the house. The gallery had been kept in good order to preserve the collections, but apart from the one room in which the captain spent almost of his time, the rest of the house, some fifty or sixty rooms, had fallen into gradual ruin. There was no mains electricity, no running water, and only one working toilet. An outbreak of dry rot had been discovered and in various parts of the house floors had been ripped up and doors taken off their hinges to examine the fungus-but the problem had not been treated and the dry rot was still creeping through the house.[91]

Pearson clearly was desperate. Though their agent gave £200,000 as a guide price for a purchase or around £6,000 as a rent (it is not clear whether that was just for the house and outbuildings but it must have been both). In the event, they let the house for twenty-one years for £250 a year and funded the insurance themselves though it was chargeable in arrears.

---

[91] *The House of New Beginnings,* Frank Wilson, Lakeland, 1977, pp. 90-91.

The drug center moved out in 1976 and the mansion and outbuildings continued their decline.

The greenhouse and Mansion

The coach house and stables

REDEVELOPMENT

In 1979, a property developer called Cavendish Holdings made a deal with the Cotswold District Council for the redevelopment of the Mansion and outbuildings with an "enabling grant" of permission to build new houses on a 35-acre plot. By 1990 Cavendish was in financial trouble and the property was taken over and completed by Clarendon Properties Limited which bargained with the District Council for more "enabling" concessions. An enabling grant is an inducement, which, in the abstract, makes sense. After World War II, England awakened to the fact that its architectural heritage was being trashed and by 1960, the government created something called "listing"–an extremely potent form of landmarking which meant that you could not alter a listed building without all sorts of vetting by various authorities. Initially, that did not mean that you could not let your listed building fall apart–you just could not work on it without permission. Northwick Mansion was listed as Grade I–very serious stuff. A few of the outbuildings were listed as Grade II which means 'ho hum–might as well keep an eye on that too'. The greenhouse was listed as Grade II*, a middle grade between I and II which means 'pretty serious'. Eventually the Cotswold District Council put the whole assemblage into a protected category all based on the Mansion's Grade I listing. The protected area restrictions are vague but the idea is that you cannot do anything that would detract from the listed building, which is why we have a hope that the fields around Northwick will remain agricultural. The law also developed rules protecting trees, so basically you can't touch many of the trees around the Mansion without having a government arborist watching and approving work. Still, all in, these heritage preservation statutes are a sensible and useful exercise of the government's police power.

This story has again and again shown loops, circles and connections in Northwick's history so it is fitting to close the story with yet another. When the redevelopers tried to get planning permission to build three houses around the fountain northwest of the Mansion, Denise Marlow, then a resident of the Gallery, brilliantly beat off the application by convincing people that there was a connection between the little fountain and Horatio Lord Nelson and Emma Hamilton, who in fact did have a connection to Lord John, the second Baron.

The file on the redevelopment in the planning office in Cirencester is really interesting. I think that what must have happened is that Ms. Marlow hired a researcher who found the connection between Lord John and the famous couple and that somehow the story got elaborated. Remarkably, someone wound up the developer's architect to the point that he wrote to the planning authorities on January 14, 1991 giving credence to the fountain being "a volcanic rock of some historical importance reputedly having been brought from Mount Vesuvius by Lord Nelson as a gift for the estate." Having made that strange admission, he goes on to explain how his siting of the proposed houses preserves the monument, *etc.* The application was rejected and an appeal ensued, which was opposed by the authorities on the grounds that evidence of the history of the garden had come to light. Everyone seems to have accepted that the fountain was volcanic stone and that the story was true. The appeal was withdrawn but I believe a deal was done because the developer was allowed to add more houses to the north including the egregiously sited "Lodge" which makes the entrance to Northwick Park so dangerous. And so the story of the Northwick-Nelson connection has taken on a life of its own.

It has been said that the fountain, now a sad pile of eroded stones, was freely copied from the Bernini fountain in Rome. We know John V wintered in Rome through the 1790s so that makes sense.

The fountain in 2005

So what was John V's connection to the famous couple to give this story some credibility?

First a few words on one of the most colorful duos in English history.

Horatio Nelson was England's greatest naval hero. He came from a middle class background, joined the English navy as a boy and spent most of his life at sea becoming an admiral and fleet commander. By the time of his first great victory, the so-called Battle of the Nile, which was actually fought off the north coast of Egypt, Nelson had already lost an arm and an eye in battle. He suffered a serious head wound in the Battle of the Nile but defeated the French Mediterranean fleet thus depriving Napoleon of control of the Mediterranean.

An additional word or two may help the modern reader understand what it meant to be a naval hero in the 17th and 18th centuries because our modern commanders are so far from the front and we have not seen a serious naval engagement since World War II. When Nelson fought the French, naval warfare consisted of something like twelve ships on each side in long rows passing each other with the attacker,

The fountain in the Victorian era

in each case Nelson, taking tremendous punishment as his lumbering ships tried to get close and broadside. Nelson actually invented a tactic which was even more punishing: he would veer into the defense line to crash through to get on their leeward side so they could be attacked from both sides at close range. The salient characteristic of all of Nelson's sea battles was to get as close as possible and slug it out. He was always on deck in the lead ship in the attack. Massive casualties were typically suffered in the approach, and by casualties I do not mean flesh wounds; I mean decapitation by cannon balls, dismemberment by flying pieces of shattered timber, being skewered by large splinters and the like. A commander like Nelson and the captains of all the ships were on deck taking their chances like everyone else in this carnage. Leading men through this meat grinder was a remarkable feat.

Nelson was truly a national hero after the Battle of the Nile but he achieved immortality in 1805 in winning the Battle of Trafalgar. Trafalgar is a bay off the coast of Cadiz, the principal Spanish Atlantic port down near Gibraltar where Nelson demolished Napoleon's fleet, thus precluding the possibility that Napoleon could invade England and establishing British naval supremacy for the 19th century. That's why he has his statue at the top of that column in Trafalgar Square in London–the most prominent monument to any one person in Britain. He was killed in the course of winning that battle by a random shot from the rigging of a French vessel with which his ship the *Victory* had faced off.[92]

Emma Hart by Romney, 1785.

Emma Hart was a very beautiful young girl who progressed from being a servant to a prostitute to a courtesan passed around a bit among the minor aristocracy. She became the mistress of a young aristocrat who after a few years had to get rid of her so that he could make a financially advantageous marriage. He literally off-loaded her on his uncle, Sir William Hamilton, the English ambassador to the Kingdom of the Two Sicilies. Sir William was an aesthete and Emma was exquisite. I have the feeling that his passion for her was in the collecting, not in the bedding, but who knows.

Emma's chief attribute was an ability to be whatever you wanted her to be or to at least act the part. She was in fact empty-headed and evolved into being self-important. Under circumstances lightly touched on below, Emma threw herself at the hero of the Nile when he came into Naples in 1798 and he, like most men dealing with a beautiful predator, did not have a chance. He was, by the time he met Emma, a physical and emotional wreck. He was only 5'6" and very slightly built with one arm, one eye, cataracts and recovering from a head wound which by some reports that had caused the skin on his forehead to fall over his eyes but that is contradicted by his surgeon's notes which read "the cranium bared for more than an inch, the wound 3" long"[93]–still pretty serious. He had always suffered from a variety of ailments (there are studies showing a remarkable pattern of great military leaders who decompensate after great battles) so all-in he was no catch except for his heroic stature. Emma was a big woman who by then had become quite stout though well-proportioned. The two of

---

[92] Today we tend to study political, social and economic history and our knowledge of geography is pitiful. You will not understand much 17th-early 20th century history without knowing a bit of military history, particularly British naval history. If you do not understand in some detail the importance of keeping the sea lanes open, you will be very much 'at sea'. Napoleon was not defeated on land for years but his ambition to be a world power ended at Trafalgar.

[93] R. Knight, *The Pursuit of Victory,* Basic Books, 2005, p. 293.

them must have cut a ridiculous figure. Their love affair ensued which became a *ménage à trois* with the aging Sir William reasonably content to share his trophy bride with Nelson whom he deeply admired. The affair was a subject of scandal and ridicule to the point that James Gillray, the acerbic political cartoonist, produced this famous print in which Sir William features as a fatuous, obtuse connoisseur and seems not to spot the pictures in the upper left of his wife (with her front porch on display) as Cleopatra beside a picture of Nelson as Mark Antony.

So that's the background.[94]

There was a connection among Lord John, Nelson and Emma. When the Republican insurgents were pressing on Naples in December 1798, Nelson, who was just in from winning the Battle of the Nile, used his ships to evacuate the King and Queen of the Two Sicilies from the northern part of the kingdom, Naples, to the southern part, Palermo. Nelson took on his flagship, the Vanguard, the King and Queen (sister of Marie Antoinette), the British ambassador to the court, Sir William Hamilton, Hamilton's wife Emma, and most of the high ranking English people who happened to be caught in Naples at the time including one John Rushout (and Louis, his valet/companion). Rushout's diary in his own hand dryly notes: "December 21 from Naples by sea at Palermo 5 day journey with Lord Nelson by the ship la Vanguard. Staid at Palermo from the 26th December to the 1 February 1799." In Palermo the Hamiltons set up house for about eighteen months and resumed their normal lavish entertaining. Emma discovered a passion for cards and sometimes staked £500 a night (an incredible sum). John Rushout is quoted as reporting "Her rage is play and Sir William says when he is dead she will be a beggar"[95] (which was prophetic). I have not found the source of the quote but it establishes that John Rushout was part of that very racy scene in Palermo.

A COGNOCENTI *contemplating y Beauties of y Antique*

James Gillray, 1801

There is more evidence of a connection, more or less in Rushout's own hand. The English intervention in the insurgency in Naples was hugely controversial to the point that some Italians still accuse the English of war crimes. The versions of who did what to whom have been written, re-written, revised, *etc.* for two hundred

---

[94] Roger Hudson, *Nelson and Emma,* ed. Folio Society, London, 1994. According to Frith, "Lord Northwick did not believe that the friendship for Lady Hamilton which Nelson professed extended beyond the bounds of ordinary friendship, and nothing made him so angry as any suggestion to the contrary." (Frith, p. 104.)

[95] *Sir William Hamilton: Envoy Extraordinary,* Brian Fothergill, Harcourt Brace, New York, 1969, p. 314.

years. The Republicans with Napoleonic assistance did capture Naples and Nelson with his squadron did eventually recapture Naples. The story is quite complex and muddy but suffice it to say that Nelson and his officers did not speak Italian, let alone Neapolitan, and John Rushout spoke Italian. There are versions of this story that have John Rushout as an attaché to the embassy headed by Sir William Hamilton but that probably just means that he was there and a bit more than a mere hanger on. At any rate, on February 9, 1846, almost half a century after the event, Rushout gave two similar versions of a couple of critical events in a statement corrected in his own hand, which are now in the British Library. He claims to have been on "terms of the greatest intimacy with Lord Nelson, the Hamiltons and all the officers of the British fleet" and to have been sent to convey the terms of surrender of Naples because he spoke Italian. He put on a British uniform and conveyed the terms. Apparently there was some confusion and Nelson was apoplectic that the terms were so liberal, so there is much finger pointing on that. Rather more importantly, the English eventually captured Commodore Francesco Caracciolo who had fought on the insurgent side and unquestionably had fired on the English and Neapolitan royal fleet. With Nelson's acquiescence, an immediate court martial of Caracciolo ensued with four Neapolitan officers and a Neapolitan president. Caracciolo was found guilty simply because he had fired. He had no counsel but his defense was one of coercion–that he was told to fight for the insurgents or be shot. Two of the trial board favored immediate execution; two favored waiting for the King to arrive and decide what to do. The president of the board favored immediate execution and Nelson agreed. Caracciolo was hanged from the yardarm of a Neapolitan vessel at five o'clock that same day. In the event, the King returned and was furious because he would have granted clemency and no one had consulted him. A serious breach of relations between the King and the English ensued and the whole incident has been debated ever since.

Rushout's statement is interesting because he manages to put everyone other than himself in a bad light. He reports that "Nelson's most distinguished officers dined at his table that day and were all against the execution & they spoke openly & strongly to Nelson on the subject. Nelson was very much agitated & threatened some of the officers for their interference." They were dining at five o'clock when Emma heard a shot and, according to Rushout, "rose from her seat with a glass of wine in her hand & holding it up said: 'Thank God! The report of that gun announces the doom of a traitor.'" Rushout repeats the story twice in his two slightly inconsistent statements. Who knows whether the statement is true but it is interesting because (a) Sir William Hamilton, the ambassador, distanced himself from the whole affair (I'm afraid that Sir William was a spineless toady but that's another story); (b) for Sir William to keep his skirts clean, Emma has to be clean and the version you read in the history books is that she swooned from her distress when the shot was heard; and (c) Emma was the friend and confidant of Queen Caroline, Marie Antoinette's sister, so of course she would be against the insurrectionists and want to punish them. Without saying so, Rushout clearly gives one the impression that Emma egged Nelson on to authorize a hanging that had very serious repercussions, thus reinforcing the version that Nelson was in Emma's thrall.[96]

It may all be rubbish–there are a lot of other reasons to believe that Rushout was an inaccurate reporter (during the same period in Italy, he reported some priests in Ischia for subversive activity; they were arrested and it was later found that Rushout's report was without

---

[96] Frith has a slightly different version of this story in his *Autobiography* pp. 104-105 but admits he is trying to record it 40 years after hearing it from Rushout.

basis). But clearly this statement does not show an old friend writing history to support his old, "intimate" friends. Maybe it is just that forty-six years later an old man wanted to distance himself from the event. Whatever, there is no question that Rushout was there and he spent a lot of time with Nelson and Emma at a critical point.

Describing the Baron's enthusiasm for Emma Hamilton, Frith recounts:

> p. 104: "'Poor dear Lady Hamilton!' he would say, in his shrill voice. 'A truer wife, a warmer friend, or a better woman never breathed'"

> p. 106: "Lord Northwick showed us every engraving that had been executed from great numbers of pictures painted from Lady Hamilton; many lovely heads by Romney among them; and many a sigh heaved the old gentleman as he produced them."

Frith goes on to observe, acidly but rightly, that Northwick did nothing for Emma when she fell into destitution after Nelson's death.

At any rate it makes perfect sense that there be a Rushout/Hamilton connection for Rushout's father had recently become a peer and Rushout himself was a very serious collector sharing William Hamilton's passion for antique artifacts and Italian painting. Sir William was the most important antiquarian of the time, having assembled, published and sold a collection of vases which became the core of the collection of the British Museum. (He most famously sold what is now called the Portland Vase.) There was every reason in the world for John and Sir William to hit it off. It is also worth noting that Sir William was a leading member of the Society of the Dilettanti (though largely *in absentia* as he served in Naples for about thirty-seven years) and John V was admitted as a member in 1802. The picture here, by Reynolds, shows Sir William (center, brown suit) performing at a meeting of the Society.

The Dilettanti Society by Reynolds, 1777.

The Dilettanti were young, wealthy, aristocratic Englishmen who had made the grand tour and acquired a taste for the antique world. Founded in 1734, the group was informal and met monthly from December to May in London. Membership was a social plum. The members had many rituals and costumes and their meetings were very well lubricated but they did sponsor some good research. John does not feature in the only extant history of the proceedings of the

Society other than the fact of his election (the author mistakenly gives the 2nd Baron the 1st Baron's c.v.)[97]

As explained above, the Hamiltons and Nelson were perhaps the most famous *ménage à trois* in modern history. During the exceedingly short periods that Nelson was on land, they all lived together with the façade of the Hamilton marriage shoring up their reputations ('just barely' to 'not at all'–they were both scandalous and ridiculous–a lethal combination). So it is entirely reasonable to infer that if John Rushout and Sir William got together, Emma and Nelson were at hand. The problem is that there is no evidence that I can find that they got together after Palermo.

When Sir William went to visit his estates in Wales after 1800, except for one well-documented trip, he traveled alone. It is perfectly reasonable to think that he would visit his young friend and, possibly, protégé, to see his collection and compare notes and Northwick is quite literally on the way between London and Southern Wales. But Northwick was in Rebecca's hands, not the Baron's, so if there was contact between Sir William and John Rushout it would probably have been at Harrow or in London.

The only time we know that Nelson and Emma were in the area was on a grand progress they made out to Wales in the summer of 1802. William and Nelson both picked up honorary degrees at Oxford[98] and the trio moved on to Woodstock where they went to Blenheim. There they were brushed off by the Duke of Marlborough who had scandals of his own to deal with and did not need the by then notorious Hamilton/Nelson set on his doorstep. The trio took varying degrees of umbrage at the slight and decamped to Burford, Cheltenham Spa, and then to Gloucester.[99]

There is no record in the secondary resources of their going to Northwick. I have looked at Nelson's principal re-printed correspondence and found nothing.[100] Fothergill makes no mention of a contact. Gill has the whole chronology of the tour almost day by day and surely a stay at Northwick for any length of time would have featured.

The only connection I can find is that Lord John acquired one of the more than a dozen Romneys of Emma, a particularly lovely one that is now in the National Portrait Gallery (NPG 4448), the same reproduced above. It is a fine picture of a beautiful woman with whom Rushout undoubtedly had some contact but Rushout bought it at "Romney's Sale" in 1834, long after the escape from Naples.[101]

---

[97] *History of the Society of Dilettanti,* Lionel Cust, Colvin, London, 1914.

[98] I wonder how many other women have seen their husband and their lover so honored on the same platform at the same time?

[99] *Nelson & the Hamiltons on Tour,* Edward Gill, Alan Sutton & Nelson Museum, 1987. See also *Nelson,* Carola Oman, Hodder & Stonghton, 1947, p. 505–a better book than most about the subject.

[100] *The Dispatches and Letters of Vice Admiral Lord Viscount Nelson,* N.H. Nicolas, 1846; I have yet to find a copy of *The Hamilton and Nelson Papers,* A. Morrison, privately printed, 1893-94.

[101] *Catalogue of the Collection of Pictures at Northwick Park, #366,* privately printed, 1921. Emma sat to Romney over 130 times; Romney's diary for 1785 is missing so it was probably much more than that. He was clearly taken with her. She sat for him twice on her wedding day, as Mrs. Hart at 9 and as Lady Hamilton at 11. (*Mid-Georgian Portraits, 1760-1790,* J. Ingamells, National Portrait Gallery, 2004.)

To me the most telling difficulty with the alleged Northwick connection is that Nelson simply did not have enough time on English soil to form one. He spent almost his entire life at sea. The Rushout/Nelson connection was formed in Naples in fall of 1798 and continued into 1799. (Nelson had been in Naples before 1798 and had met the Hamiltons but no sparks flew– Nelson was not yet the hero of the Nile.) Nelson was in England November 6, 1800 to January 26, 1801 when he headed for what became the Battle of Copenhagen. In October 1801 Nelson was home. In the summer of 1802 the trio toured the West Country and then he was in London until April 1803. He embarked for the Mediterranean in May of 1803 and returned to England on August 18, 1805 then headed for Trafalgar on September 14, 1805, where he was killed. There just was no time for a prolonged association with Northwick.

So the fountain myth is a great story and it did the trick. So we close with yet another circle in Northwick's history; an innocent fable rooted in Northwick's past which served to protect its future.

APPENDIX I

The Legal Context

The history of English real property law helps explain some of the dynamics that shaped Northwick and basically kept it in the hands of two families for about seven hundred years.

First, a word of caution. English legal history emerges from the study of little snippets in court records which describe in a few words the positions of the parties and the result in the case. From these shards historians conclude that at any point in time the law recognized some claims of right but not others. That is–Richard Roe sued John Doe complaining that Doe did something and if the court did not say Doe was wrong, that suggests that in law as they understood, Roe had no claim. This analytic process is fraught both because of the lack of data and because it is extremely difficult to discern patterns of legal principle in these snippets. But it becomes even worse when the court's conclusion is that a claim is upheld or lost because of a controlling custom which is not described. While there were legal treatises written before the middle of the 17th century, they are extremely difficult to follow and not uniformly recognized as being entirely correct.

The fundamental concept of English property law is that after 1066, every square inch of land in England was owned by the King so all rights to possess land were within the King's gift. The King needed three things: (1) a mechanism to exercise control over a large, sparsely populated territory where travel was difficult at best; (2) a source of revenue because the King personally funded all functions of government; and (3) a thriving agricultural economy to produce wealth and maintain social stability. The structure that evolved to meet these needs is now called feudalism, the central feature of which was that the King granted control over vast tracts of land to a small number of individuals who in turn owed him a duty of loyalty and the obligation to govern and produce revenue. They were tenants of the King and in turn they divided the possessory rights to their estates among others who became their tenants with similar rights and duties. Those tenants in turn sublet to others until the actual possession of the land was in the hands of the agricultural workers who produced the wealth. The larger tenants had the right and duty to govern and one of their chief functions was to run courts to deal with most civil and the lesser criminal offenses. These larger tenancies were generally called manors; the chief tenant was the lord of the manor and his court and court officers were the mechanism of control. I repeatedly use the word 'tenant' to highlight the fact that all interests in land were subject to the rights of the King; no one other than the King could own any property absolutely. As a practical matter, however, to foster economic growth and production, security of tenure is required–no sensible farmer is going to sow a crop if he can be evicted by his landlord just before the crop is harvested–so over about five hundred years rather complex rules developed which gave differing degrees of security of tenure, including the right to buy and sell land and the right to dispose of it by will.

Originally the tenants owed services to their landlords. For example, a tenure known as knights service was conditioned on the tenant providing a properly equipped knight to the King for forty days a year but as society and warfare became more complex, the King really could not run a war with a pick-up army where the soldiers went home after forty days. Therefore the obligation was commuted into paying a monetary rent, which the King used to raise more permanent forces. The same sort of commutation occurred with the other forms of medieval tenancy and, most importantly, to provide security of tenure, the rents tended to become fixed so with inflation or depreciation of the currency over time, the rents became unimportant or nominal or were not even collected. As a result the concept of something resembling what we think of as outright ownership became stronger.

The King still needed revenue, however, so he still insisted on his periodic feudal rights which included the obligation of a tenant to pay a fee to pass his estate by will, another fee for the heir to inherit, and very lucrative fees to manage the affairs of orphans or grant permission for a woman to marry. All of these royal prerogatives seem abusive in our eyes but they all have at their root the bedrock principle that all land is within the gift of the King. If the King grants a farm to X and X dies, the King is entitled to get the farm back and keep it for his own use or give it to someone else so if X wants to pass it to his child and the child wants to keep it, they should pay the King to induce him not to exploit his opportunity to make another use of the farm. Guardianship and the right to control who a woman marries also seem to have been justified by the theory that the lord has the right to raise the orphan as a suitable tenant and to make sure the woman does not introduce an undesirable tenant to the estate as her property became the property of her husband upon marriage. These rights continued until 1660 but even after that, the property of a felon was forfeit to the King upon conviction and estates with no claimant (*e.g.* no surviving family) reverted to the King.

A key to maintaining the stability of this system was to be sure that control was held by a small group of people since, given the geographical and staffing obstacles, the King was incapable of effective central administration. Keeping control in the hands of a few was the impulse behind primogeniture–the absolute requirement that real property interests pass to the eldest child (in England almost always male with rare exceptions). This strict legal requirement kept the big estates from being broken up and it was not until 1540 that the option of passing a real property interest to someone else by will was created. At around the same time, the lawyers devised a purely fictional lawsuit as a method of breaking entailment, a restriction imposed by a grantor that the property pass only to an eldest son or daughter. You will see all these forces at work at Northwick, and see again and again just how few and inter-related the great landowners of England were–all the product of a legal system created to promote prosperity through the controlled devolution of limited property rights in aid of governance by an understaffed and under-funded central government.

APPENDIX II

Enclosure

Northwick's having grown by enclosure perhaps justifies a digression into this subject. Over hundreds of years, the size and configuration of plots of land in England both privately held and for common use became increasingly inefficient for agricultural development and stymied investment. The root motivation of what became known as enclosure was to aggregate parcels for efficient agricultural use.

Though patterns of land tenure were not uniform over England, generally very large tracts were deemed available for use in common. The overlay in 1066 of the legal concept that all land is held by grant from the King had little to do with possession; it simply created a new landlord for those in possession. In fact the rights and duties of parties continued in large part according to local custom and as such varied tremendously over the country. So while legally, at least after 1066, the lord controlled the common areas, his use of it was severely constrained by custom.

Not only agricultural land was held in common; woodlots and quarries were as well. As to the agricultural land, some was held for pasture with strict rules as to who could pasture what, where and when and some was parceled out to individuals to be cropped. The cropped parcels were separated from one another by strips of unplowed land with no other boundaries because every few years the cropped land was put to pasture and the former pasture cropped. Even more importantly, animals were allowed to graze on cropped land outside of the planting and growing season. This enforced rotation discouraged individuals from trying anything new such as planting earlier or later or upgrading the soil in their plot.

For some reason, the individual plots were long and narrow—as much as 260 yards long. Perhaps this was because it is difficult to turn an ox-drawn plow so going straight for as long as possible is preferable. For whatever reason, the plots were small—maybe half an acre. Two acres was big. Individuals were given multiple non-contiguous strips perhaps so that everyone got good bits, so-so bits and not very good bits or because of the practice of field rotation. For whatever reason, the result discouraged individual experiment and investment and it has been persuasively argued that the land deteriorated over the years and became so non-productive that the serfs simply could not make a living, starting to move off the land even before the bubonic plague which wiped out as much as 40% of the population of England between 1348 and 1350.[102] The Black Death must have forced a change in land use and tenure as there were fewer people to work the land and then resulted in another change as the country re-populated itself by 1600. The new people had to go somewhere to live and work, but other than showing the trends, the data does not furnish proof of causation.

Enclosure began before 1500 and there are arguments that it was half over by then but from the records, we can see a lot of enclosure occurring in the 17th century. Originally enclosure was arranged by private agreement among the parties concerned; by the 18th century and well into the 19th century, it was done by act of Parliament on a case-by-case basis. Petitions would be filed

---

[102] *The Enclosures in England: An Economic Reconstruction,* Harriett Bradley, 1918, Batoche Books reprint 2001.

(usually by the wealthy landowners who had the most to gain and could fund the effort) but, when allowed, the required process was that expert valuers and surveyors developed a plan under which it was attempted to give everyone their share of the right sort of land–you got as good as you gave up–but in a rational and arable pattern. Certainly by the 19th century this was a very professional and carefully supervised activity. The financial costs of the work, which included surveying and marking out the new tracts, had to be paid pro-rata by the landowners involved. Then there was the requirement that the new tract had to be fenced or hedged, which was the real problem for the small holders who might have been given a much more valuable piece of land in trade but could not afford to pay their share of the project costs and certainly could not pay for the fencing or hedging. The result was a lot of land transfers and forced sales.[103]

Starting with Karl Marx himself (*Capital*, Vol. I, Ch. 27), the enclosures have often been interpreted as class warfare with the rich grinding the faces of the poor. For hundreds of years there have been horror stories of farmers forced off their land as their crops were maturing. Some of this must be true. It is also true that there were riots and even a local peasant revolt in the early 17th century linked to the enclosures. Yet often one need read only a paragraph of an historical publication on the enclosures to have a very clear idea of the social and political views of the author. I wonder whether accounts of a few riots and some very emotive letters are enough to judge the impact of a process that took five hundred years. The data simply are not good enough to know the social consequences. Clearly the large landowners and the Church did well because they had the funds and presumably ended up with more efficient and therefore valuable holdings.

There is not yet sufficient data to reach confident conclusions about the enclosures. We do not really know why the notion of owning land in common evolved as it did, so why do we think we really know why it ended; this is all a matter of making shrewd, informed guesses. As Bradley demonstrated almost a hundred years ago, most of the theories such as wool becoming more valuable than crops so the rich wanted to create pastures do not hold up. But why should there be one or two predominant reasons that something happened over five hundred years in a country as tradition bound as England? My own sense of it is that it took five hundred years for people rooted in custom from time immemorial to realize that the structural limitations imposed by common ownership were not working out for them. Having the whole community in lock-step in agricultural practices probably did deplete the soil causing the serfs to leave (or die). That, coupled with the plague and the rise of cities and manufacturing in the 17th century, probably came together in different ways in different times and places to force change in something as conservative as land use.[104]

---

[103] *Enclosure Records for Historians,* Steven Hollowell, Phillimore, 2000.

[104] For more insights see *The New Reading the Landscape,* Richard Muir, University of Exeter Press, 2000.

APPENDIX III

Rebecca's Letters to Hastings

Northwick Park
February 17th 1806

Dear Mr Hastings
Altho' I am always extremely delighted to see your handwriting, I cannot help being very, very anxious at the account you give me of my Dear Friend Mrs Hastings. I will hope the indisposition you mention was of short continuance & that she is now perfectly recovered–I hardly dare to think of our Political Situation, much less talk of it, because I am ignorance itself;–I wish however I could see the Prospect in the same chearful [sic] point of view with yourself;–I must still dread an Invasion while B_P_ has such an army, elated by Conquest & success, the total silence that now seems to prevail at Paris, rather increases my fears, instead of lessening them. He will speak in thunder when he is prepared, may the Almighty protect us, he only can–
I feel greatly for our excellent King, his mortifications must be great, & call for all his fortitude. God grant he may not sink under his trials–I rejoice must sincerely in Lord Coventry's recovery. I have may obligations to him, both as an excellent Neighbor & most valuable friend–
Adieu my Dear Sir. I hope soon to hear that my Dear Mrs Hastings is in perfect health:–that you m[ay] both long enjoy your present happ[iness] is the sincere wish of
Your much obliged & faithful.
R Northwick
[Letters in brackets are added as a bit of the page is missing.]

Northwick Park February 27, 1806
Many thanks my Dear Sir for your very kind & agreeable letter, doubly welcome, because it brought me so good an account of my Dear Mrs Hastings, & because your minds seems to be satisfied with the conduct of the Directors of the Company who owe you so much attention–I have a favor to ask, which is that you will give your support and Interest in the Neighborhood of Daylesford to my Friend Mr Lygon who stands as a Candidate for the County of Worcester in succeed his father–
Lady Beauchamp & one of her sons Dined with my on her way to Madresfield on Monday last & then all was quiet & no opposition expected, but alas we now have two opponents–My Lyttelton & Mr Biddulph have both offered, & tho' I flatter myself they have no chance of success, yet they may give a great deal of trouble,–I hope Mr Lygon who is a most worthy & amiable young man (supported by Lord Coventry who is very zealous in the cause) need not fear–Here we are all unanimous & I have the pleasure to think that my being in the Country at this time has been of some service–
The Weather at times is quite charming & the Birds sing as they do in May, these delights I fear will not yet tempt you into the County, but whereever you are may Health & Happiness attend you both, is the sincere prayer of
Your obliged & affectionate
R Northwick

* * *

In a letter simply dated March 1806 but probably before the 7th as that is the date of the next letter in the binder, she reports to Hastings a "comical incident" that happened the prior week when Mr Lyttleton came by unannounced. "After the first salutation was over, he said 'Well, you have all done me a great deal of Mischief I believe & <u>you</u> in particular,' addressing himself to <u>me</u>– I told him I was [illegible] to find he had so much charity as not to bear malice & that I was glad to see him–He then began to ridicule & abuse all the House of Lygon in very gross terms, till I found myself obliged to check him & to say that I really could not submit to hear my friends treated in so improper a manner, however witty it might be–he stayed here till late the next day & early in the morning following Lady Beauchamp called here on her way to London & I felt very happy that the two Rivals did not meet–"

On July 18, 1806 she writes from Wanstead Grove where she has been for she does not enjoy London "as it is <u>now</u>." "I should rarely see it, if I had not Duties to perform which make it <u>necessary</u>. I have been at this sweet Place near a fortnight & am much better for the [illegible] quite I enjoy."

* * *

Northwick Park
February 27, 1808
"Indeed my Dear Sir I feel most sensibly your kindness in writing to me at this time. I might and should have written to my Dear Mrs Hastings long ago, but my own health & spirits have been so very indifferent that I have not had courage to take my Pen in hand…My dearest Harriet [her daughter] was so very indifferent when she left me, both in health & spirits, that I have been in terrors for her ever since & a very severe [illegible] of 80 [?] miles through very bad Roads covered with snow, in a [illegible] carriage of Mr Cockerells which broke down with them & and left them waiting on the Road near two hours before they could get another carriage from Oxford,–all this added to the fatigues[?] of Body & Mind near [?] too much for her gentile spirits, & she was extremely ill at White Knights. I hope she is now pretty well & that the Bridal Happiness may continue without alloy of any kind. I have only to wish she may be as <u>happy</u> as she deserves. C'est [illegible] dire! All this is in confidence & only to be mentioned to dear Mrs Hastings.
How do you like this severe [?] cold Weather. I have hardly courage to face the cold air, but am contented with my comfortable chimney corner, & a small Circle of good friends. My brother in [law?], also my son George & Lady Caroline Rushout with her <u>three</u> sweet babes,–they are charming Children & the two oldest very amusing,–the youngest is the prettiest Babe I ever saw, but at this time suffering most cruelly from his teeth, indeed so much so as to alarm us extremely–may God preserve him!!"

* * *

27 August 1807
"I see by the Papers that the Prince of Wales is now at Cheltenham. I have no doubt but that he will pay his [illegible] at Daylesford. I beg and beseech you my Dear Mr Hastings to permit me to supply with Venison & Pine apples which are the only things I believe in my power to offer, which Daylesford does not produce in much greater perfection than N. Park." [She is not cadging an invitation–she is on a tour in the Welsh mountains with "my little companions" and won't get to Northwick before the Prince's visit.]

* * *

Undated letter

Thanks Hastings for letter giving "so much information upon a subject so near my Heart. I have so many obligations to our good & excellent King & have received so many favors from him at various times that I must rejoice at all that can give him comfort & pleasure. May he soon recover this severe blow [?] which seems to be occasioned by the feelings of a tender Heart!"

* * *

Undated letter
"And now my Dear Sir I must thank you for your generous proposal of sending me some of your beautiful seed wheat. I can only accept it upon the usual terms <u>We</u> <u>Farmers</u> always adopt, that is, mutual <u>exchange</u> but by <u>this</u> you would be the great loser, for your wheat is very fine & mine is very indifferent, but if you will accept half a Buck in <u>exchange</u>, I shall gladly thank you for six bushel, & will send a man & horse for it, the latter end of this month. I will beg you the favor of you to write a line to my keeper when you wish to have the Venison & I have ordered Wm. Allcock to obey your commands."

* * *

Another undated letter
She says is delayed in responding because she has had a party of fourteen at dinner and has to decline some invitation because "I am engaged to Lady Redesdale [Batsford] on Friday & must attend her christening. I therefore hope you will kindly postpone your visit til <u>Saturday</u> when I hope & trust you will be at leisure to pass some days with me, the longer the better."

* * *

Another undated letter
Says she was delayed in responding to a letter and would have responded "had not a severe cold affected my powers of holding a Pen." Repeats herself commenting on Mrs Hastings' poor health and hoping she is better. Complains repeatedly of the North East Wind.

APPENDIX IV

The South Sea Bubble

In which I try to make interesting the problems of funding England's national debt.

The Funding Problem

The Crown had to pay for wars, which are expensive, and the Crown had limited sources of revenue.

Kings borrowed on their personal responsibility and when they died, their heirs did not necessarily pay their debts. Charles II simply told the Exchequer in 1672 not to pay principal on most of his debts, which amounted to making his creditors give him a forced loan at 6%, which ruined a large number of them.

Charles II died owing over a million pounds, which largely was never paid.

The Crown's obligations to pay tended to trade at a discount, both because of uncertainty as to whether they would ever be paid, and because they were illiquid. It was not until 1693 that Parliament began guaranteeing Crown debt, but even then the Crown's promissory notes were not negotiable and could not be exchanged at the Exchequer for notes in smaller principal amounts to facilitate payment of smaller debts–you had to hold the notes to maturity and hope that you would get your semi-annual promised interest payments in the meantime.

In the latter part of the 17ᵗʰ century the money supply began to expand from gold and silver, in part because there simply was not enough specie to fund the expanding economy. Goldsmiths' notes were accepted as short-term credit and traded pretty nearly as cash. Merchant bankers facilitated trade by making promises (called bills of exchange) to each other to pay, and as portfolios of promises built up in corresponding currencies and maturities, the bankers offset their mutual obligations on agreed terms. Even the Exchequer began issuing interest-bearing notes that functioned like currency.

The Crown funded itself in part by selling privileges. The Stuarts sold over three thousand baronetcies, with Charles II being the most active seller at £1,095 each. (That would be about £100,000 in 2005; James I bought one.) The East India Company paid the government handsomely for its charter and exclusive trading rights and also lent the government a lot of money to stay in favor. The first vehicle created primarily to fund government debt was the Bank of England. The Bank was privately owned but chartered by the Crown in 1694, with the authority to act as an intermediary for the Exchequer, which lacked the staff to issue, transfer and pay its own obligations in any volume. The Bank issued its own obligations indirectly secured by the Crown's corresponding obligation to pay the Bank 8% on the Bank's £1.2 million capital, which was lent to the Crown. By 1697, the Bank was authorized to raise another £1 million in capital with which to acquire Crown obligations on which the government agreed to continue to pay interest and to redeem over a period of time. Thus was established the pattern that a private corporation would raise capital, acquire government obligations with the proceeds and reschedule the debt with the Crown.

The Bank's notes were also attractive because they were transferable on the books of the Bank–far easier than transfers through the Exchequer. Yet that was not enough to fund the ever-growing Crown debt, which the War of the Spanish Succession increased to £9.5 million by 1710. A lot of that debt was short-term and bore interest rates up to 10% while suffering from the same liquidity problems. The Bank alone could not manage the debt, though it had a monopoly to do so. Help was at hand.

The South Sea Company is Created

Three very sharp men had acquired the corporate charter of the Hollow Sword Blade Company, which had been created in 1691 with the limited authority to forge sword blades with a curved groove down their lengths. Such weapons theretofore had only been available on the Continent.

By 1703 these clever guys took Sword Blade out of the blade-forging business and instead, in violation of its charter, used it to acquire confiscated Jacobite estates in Ireland, thereby allowing the Crown to reduce some of its debt by selling surplus property it did not want. Sword Blade then became a lender in competition with the Bank. This was arguably an infringement on the Bank's government-granted monopoly rights and was clearly a violation of the terms of Sword Blade's charter, but the government looked the other way when the Bank protested, probably because Sword Blade was another vehicle to help manage government debt. The government's tolerance paid off.

The government had in recent years tried to re-fund its short-term debt with the proceeds of lotteries managed by the Bank. The Bank's record as a lottery runner was not very good and it was having trouble with its latest effort. In 1711 the principals of Sword Blade basically took over and organized the first successful state lottery to raise funds desperately needed for the War of the Spanish Succession. On the back of this success, the Sword Blade promoters of the lottery got Parliament to authorize the organization of South Sea Company to mop up £9.5 million of government debt which had no dedicated revenue source to service it.

The promoters' scheme was a hybrid of the Bank of England's role as an intermediary in servicing and rescheduling public debt and the East India Company's speculation in trade. The Company would, in effect, reschedule Crown debt while giving creditors who accepted the rescheduled debt an equity kicker–a shareholder's capital interest in a company with have an exclusive monopoly to trade into the Spanish territories in Central and South America, a region then known as the South Sea. The trading operation was purely speculative because the War of the Spanish Succession would not be over for three years, but the sales pitch was that the Crown was promising that if and when it beat the Spanish, it would exact the trading monopoly as part of the treaty terms and hand the monopoly over to the South Sea Company.

The South Sea Company was an attractive investment and immediately 97% of the Crown's illiquid short-term, high interest notes (then trading on average at a 32% discount) were tendered for South Sea shares which were backed by the government's promise to pay the Company 6% of each share's £100 par value lent to the government.

The long-term debt holders tendered as well even though their debt usually had interest rates of 7% and the Company shares they got only yielded 5% backed by the government annuity. Some of the exchanged long-term debt had fixed maturities which traded at discount because of uncertainty of payment and difficulty of transfer and some were life annuities which added the burden of proving twice a year that you were alive (usually by a note from your priest or a notary) so you could collect your interest. The holders of life annuities could convert to a fixed term by paying an additional premium and they did so and then converted to Company shares. In each case, tendering seems to have been a sensible choice.

Between 1715 and 1719 the government carried out several of these conversion offers in which the Company participated by accepting government debt in payment for new government-authorized additional shares. In this period, Company stock bumped around but eventually got up to £114/share.

The business flaw in the scheme was that the bonus of trading into the Spanish South Sea possession never really prospered. The first problem was that in the final settlement with Spain, England only got limited access to the South Sea market. It got the right to sell 4,800 black slaves a year plus make one 500-ton shipment of trading goods. Even cheating by slipping contraband trade goods in with the slaves did not make that trade successful. Secondly, and probably more importantly, no one in the Company knew anything about foreign trade and no one cared to learn. The Company promoters were financial guys; the trade aspect was a sales gimmick. It's not that they didn't try–the company had a fleet, port facilities, *etc.*–it simply lacked a viable business plan.

That said, a poor business plan was not the fatal structural flaw in the South Sea house of cards. The bubble occurred because the Company was authorized to issue shares equal at par value to the debts surrendered. If the Company could induce the buyers to pay over par, the Company would have the excess authorized shares in its treasury which it could use or sell for other purposes. Thus, if the current market for Company shares was £128 and the Company was authorized to issue £10 million of shares at par £100, it could issue the shares for £7,801,500 and have £2,198,750 in treasury shares to invest in other things or to create mischief.

Eventually in 1720, the Company offered to reschedule the Crown's entire £31 million remaining debt. The Company had to compete with the Bank to get the assignment. To close the deal with the government, the Company gave bribes noted in a so-called "Green Book" in which forty to fifty influential people, including a cabinet minister, were noted to have subscribed for shares they did not pay for. As the shares appreciated, the favored few were allowed to sell to pay for the shares they nominally subscribed for and pocket the profit. The bribes were even given to George I's two mistresses, the "fat one" and the "thin one", as part of the necessary hype was to show that the great and the good (or not so good) were behind the scheme. George I personally held £60,000 in Company shares at par value but very few people really knew what was going on; most of the Company directors did not have a clue. Almost no one knew about the Green Book which, unsurprisingly, has never been found.

The stock began to rise on the rumors that the issue of new stock would be approved by the government. The issuance was approved there ensued a series of seven subscription offers between April 14, 1720 and August 24, 1720. The first was for cash (not debt) at £300/share on attractive terms–20% down, balance in 10% installments at two-month intervals. The second for long-term and short-term annuities went out at £375/share. The third was for cash at £400/share. Obviously the message to the market was to get on board for immediate capital gains. The next subscription at £1,000/share on June 17, 1721 was for cash, not debt, with 10% down and the balance in 10% increments at six-month intervals after an initial year without payments, so you had over five years to pay in full while you hoped for capital gain. From an investor's point of view, a 5% dividend on a £100 par share was a yield of ½ of 1% if he bought at £1000/share, but since he only paid £100 down, he was still getting 5% until he had to make the next payment in a year when his yield would drop to 2.5% on his cash. Those investors had to see capital appreciation or they were wiped out. To prop up the price, the Company lent funds to shareholders so that they could buy more Company stock–typically if you had 100 shares at par value you could borrow £250. As time went on, the Company began to lend the government money and even pay premiums to the government to receive the authority to issue more stock.

There was an element of a Ponzi scheme involved. To hype the shares, the Company not only made loans, it increased its promises of dividends without an ability to pay them because it had so little cash. Cash had to come from new subscriptions garnered by promises of increased dividends which the Company could not pay.

An important effect of this scheme was that it sucked money out of the economy to chase profits. The profits that were realized increased inflation and the prices of luxury goods in particular rose dramatically. People with paper profits spent like mad.

All this occurred in a very frothy market. As many as 190 stock promotions were launched after September 1719. By June 11, 1721, the "Bubble Act" formally entitled an "Act to Restrain the Extravagant and Unwarrantable Practices of Raising Money by Voluntary Subscriptions for Carrying on Projects Dangerous to the Trade and Subjects of the Kingdom", had achieved royal assent–but the damage had been done.

The bubble burst in 1720 in what had elements of a perfect storm. Most importantly, John Law's management of the French financial system which had created massive inflation and wild speculation began to collapse in 1719. Flight capital from France flowed into Company stock. As the French economy collapsed, English and Dutch investors who were heavily into the French market saw their profits and indeed their assets disappear along those of the French, who were also heavily in the English market, including Company stock. The Company's shares peaked at £1050 on June 24, 1720 but its stock offerings began to be less well-received as credit evaporated and everyone wanted gold or silver currency. The stock dropped like a rock down to £155/share on December 15, 1720 while smaller bubbles were bursting all over the market.

Unquestionably a lot of investors were ruined or reduced to straightened circumstances. A lot more who thought they were rich and had spent accordingly had their paper profits, sense of well-being and self-esteem evaporate. But the Company survived because the government annuity was still paid. If you had bought the shares at less than £126 and just held them, you were okay.

The Company's South Sea trade fizzled out in the 1740s. The Company was restructured by the government and because the government annuities supporting the shares had such long maturities, the Company became simply a clearinghouse for interest on the government debt to the shareholders. Every English sovereign from George I through Victoria became the Governor of the Company, an honorary position, until 1854 when the last annuity was paid. The Company was dissolved in 1855.

The main effect of the bust was that there were no vibrant financial markets in England for over a hundred years. It was only the industrial revolution and the development of railroads that revived the animal spirits.

The received wisdom about the South Sea Bubble is that it ranks with the tulip mania of the late 17th century as a prime example of the madness of crowds. Not really. The South Sea Company was sponsored and nurtured by the government to reduce the national debt. Yes, it was helped along by graft and corruption and a frothy market in other highly speculative ventures—but the Company was an instrument of government policy and could have functioned perfectly well as an intermediary rescheduling government debt.

In the aftermath, a handful of directors and government ministers had almost all their assets seized after parliamentary investigations and for the most part rightly so. But the real lesson was that almost no one understood that this basically rather clever way of managing the government debt and increasing liquidity in the newborn financial markets needed oversight and internal controls.

The nearest modern parallel I can think of is America's housing and finance vehicle Fannie Mae and its cohorts–privately owned but government sponsored to promote homeownership with all its good effects. Not a bad idea at all but particularly when the politicians saw that they could get political credit for homeownership expansion by pushing the institution to take more risks, eventually the wheels came off. It is not a lesson on the madness of crowds; it is a lesson in the willful blindness of governments and occasional corruption of politicians.

BIBLIOGRAPHY

I decided not to burden the text with scholarly footnotes and references to files in libraries and archives. I am happy to try to help other researchers who want to know where the bodies are buried. Where I quoted directly from someone else's work in the text, I gave a citation, some of which are duplicated below. These are a few of the more important works I stole from shamelessly. Now thanks to Google Books you can download most of them, thereby saving yourself the time and travel expense that it cost me to find them. But you won't have the profound pleasure of searching in some of the world's great archives and libraries, which is too bad for you.

Blockley Through Twelve Centuries, H.C.M. Icely, Blockley Heritage Society, 1988.

The History of Blockley, A.J. Soden, Coventry, 1875.

Raising Spirits, Making Gold and Swapping Wives, Michael Wilding, Shoestring Press, 1999. (the John Dee connection)

The Land Laws, Frederick Pollock Macmillan (reprinted by Elibron Classics), 1883.

The History of Parliament: The House of Commons 1660-1690, B.D. Henning, ed. HMSO.

The Heraldry of Worcestershire, John Russell Smith, 1873.

English East India Company, KN Chaudhuri Routledge/Thoenimes Press (Digital Version 2002).

A Treatise on the Law Relating to Aliens and Denization and Naturalization, George Hansard, London, 1844.

Knights of England, Vol. II, W.A. Shaw, Sherratt and Hughes, London, 1906.

Harrow School and Its Surroundings, P. Thornton, Allen & Co., 1885.

A History of the Levant Company, A.C. Wood, Frank Carrs & Co., 1964 (reprint of 1935 edition).

R. Wittoker, 'Lord Burlington at Northwick Park' in H. Colvin & J. Harris (eds.), *The Country Seat,* 1970.

Inventories of Worcestershire Landed Gentry 1537-1786, M. Wankly, Ed. Worcestershire Historical Society, 1998.

The History of Parliament, The House of Commons, 1715-54, Romney Sedgwick, ed. HMSO.

The Pursuit of Victory, R. Knight, Basic Books, 2005.

Sir William Hamilton: Envoy Extraordinary, Brian Fothergill, Harcourt Brace, New York, 1969.

Blockley Yesterday: A Third Blockley Miscellany, privately printed, 2000.

My Autobiography and Reminiscences, W.P. Frith, Harper, New York, 1888.

History of the Society of Dilettanti, Lionel Cust, Colvin, London, 1914.

Nelson & the Hamiltons on Tour, Edward Gill, Alan Sutton & Nelson Museum, 1987.

Nelson, Carola Oman, Hodder & Stoughton, 1947.

Sir Robert Clayton and the Origins of English Deposit Banking 1658-1685, Frank T. Melton, Cambridge University Press, 1986.

Records of the Bowles Family: Being the History of a Line Deriving from Charles Bowles of Chatham During Three Centuries: With Annotated Pedigrees of the Parent House of Swineshead and Haugh, and of the Cadet Families Settled in Lincolnshire, Nottinghamshire, and Kent. William Henry Bowles, Derby, London, 1918.

Eighteenth-Century English Politics, Robert A. Smith, Holt, Rinehart and Winston, 1972.

The South Sea Bubble, John Carswell, Stanford University Press, 1960.

The Rise of Financial Capitalism, Larry Neal, Cambridge University Press, 1990.

SOURCES OF IMAGES

The contemporary pictures of Northwick, Blockley and Chipping Campden are by the author except as noted in the text.

The locations of paintings from museums are as noted.

The bronze bull is © Trustees of the British Museum.

John Rushout's Letters Patent are in The National Archives of the United Kingdom.

The Rushout family portrait was computer enhanced from a rather poor photograph in the Christies sale catalogue for the "Northwick Park" Important English Pictures c. 1550–c. 1880 Friday, June 25, 1965 sale. The photographer A.C. Cooper reported that it gave the negatives to Christies and Christies reported that its archive was flooded so this may be the best image currently available.

The Emes drawing and prints of Anne Rushout's paintings are in the Yale Center for British Art Library.

The 1783 view of Northwick is in the British Library © The British Library Board. Maps K.Top.43.77

The details of the 1819 map and the Rushout pedigree are in the Worcestershire Records Office (a/k/a Worcestershire Archive and Archaeology Service).

The three Rushout Girls are in the Huntington Library. © Courtesy of the Huntington Art Collections, San Marino, California.

The miniature of Anne Rushout is in the Royal Ontario Museum.

Other images were found on the web.

DRAMATIS PERSONÆ: THE RUSHOUTS

John I	(1593-1653)	The immigrant from Flanders
John II	(1629-1648)	Died in a fall from a horse
James I	(1643-1697)	Purchased Northwick; built west front and greenhouse
James II	(1667-1705)	Son of James I and Alice
James III	(1705-1711)	Son of James II and Arabella
John III	(1685-1775)	Son of James II, uncle of James III
		Employed Burlington; Father of House of Commons
John IV	(1738-1800)	First Baron
John V	(1769-1859)	Second Baron
		The collector
George I	(1772-1887)	Third Baron